Six New Gospels

SIX NEW GOSPELS
NEW TESTAMENT WOMEN TELL
THEIR STORIES

MARGARET HEBBLETHWAITE

COWLEY PUBLICATIONS

Published in the United States of America by Cowley Publications, a division of the Society of St John the Evangelist. No portion of this book may be reproduced, stored in or introduced into a retrieval system, or transmitted, in any form or by any means – including photocopying – without the prior written permission of Cowley Publications, except in the case of brief quotations embodied in critical articles and reviews.

Published in Great Britain by Geoffrey Chapman, a Cassell imprint.

First published 1994
Reprinted 1994

Library of Congress Cataloging-in Publication Data is available from the Library of Congress, or from Cowley Publications upon request.

ISBN: 1–56101–087–1

Cover picture: Caroline Mackenzie, *Three Women at the Empty Tomb*. Oil on canvas. © Caroline Mackenzie.

Typeset by Colset Private Ltd, Singapore
Printed and bound in Great Britain by
Biddles Ltd, Guildford and King's Lynn

Cowley Publications
28 Temple Place
Boston, Massachusetts 02111

CONTENTS

INTRODUCTION

In this book I look at Jesus through the eyes of women. But because women are so different, and there is no single perspective that can be labelled 'the woman's view', I look at Jesus six times, through the eyes of six different women. In effect that gives us what might be called six new gospels, each written from a different woman's viewpoint, each re-told in a fictional form and in the first person.

But the book can be read at two levels, both metaphorically and literally, because in continuous commentary on the story-line there is an ample subtext of theological footnotes. Here I give references, explanations and additional reflections. And so throughout, two texts can be read: the story, and the theological commentary. It may be best to read the story all through once before being delayed by the notes. No one is obliged to read both at once, or indeed, to read both at all.

Who are the six women? There is Mary of Nazareth, of course, the mother of Jesus, about whom we have more scriptural material than any other woman. There is Mary of Magdala, whom all four gospels appear to recognize as the leading woman disciple. There are Martha and Mary of Bethany, the two sisters who figure in the gospels of Luke and John, and whose home Jesus made so much his own. There is Elizabeth, the mother of John the Baptist, around whom Luke weaves such a gracious story in the early chapters of his gospel. And there is the woman whom Jesus met at a well in Samaria, whose conversation with Jesus is lengthy and probing: John's gospel gives her no name, but I have followed an ancient tradition in calling her Photina.

What about the unnamed woman who anoints Jesus in Matthew and Mark? Or the 'sinner' who anoints him in Luke? Here I have followed John's gospel in identifying the woman of the anointing incident as Mary of Bethany. The more familiar tradition that she was Mary Magdalene is now totally discredited.

What about the woman bent double? Or the woman taken in adultery? Or the woman with the issue of blood? Or the disciple who came from Herod's court, Joanna? I could not write about everyone, but chose those for whom there was the most material to start from. In every case, of course, we are working from fragments, because women have been systematically overlooked in the traditions that have come down to us, so that there are only a few original stones in the mosaic we try to reconstruct.

My work of reconstruction does not aim to be rigidly bound by history, for I have incorporated a hint of what might be called 'modern dress'. My characters express their experience, from time to time, through the concepts which modern women would use, rather than through ones that women of that era might have used. And so they speak, for example, of eating sandwiches and talking theology, of staying in hotels and doing pastoral work, rather than of eating bread and fish and discussing law, of staying in inns and doing the work of the Lord. I have tried in short to make a thoroughly modern translation, avoiding terms that are culturally alien from women of today, so as to enable these figures from the past to speak to their modern sisters and brothers with maximum immediacy and relevance.

The search for a mere historical reconstruction would in any case be an impossible one. For a long time now scripture scholarship has rejected the method of conflating the different gospels to produce a synthesized account, because that approach seemed locked into an impossible search for the historical Jesus. Attention centred rather around the differing intentions of the four evangelists, and the various influences of Church and society on the way each of them adapted their material. If we could never recover the original facts, we could at least explore the later stages of adaptation.

But if we now address feminist questions to the scriptures we find ourselves wrestling with questions of methodology all over again. We are not content with illumining the intentions of the evangelists, because the evangelists intended to write a male-dominated story. Nor are we content with considering the interests and influences of the early Church communities, because they tended towards the same assumption that women's place was out of sight. What interests us about the gospels is not so much what has been left in, but what has been left out. We are looking for the suppressed role of women. But what has been left out is now irrecoverable, like a file deleted from a computer. How then can we proceed?

There appear to be two ways forward. One is to make the most of the little that we have. That means paying close attention to the limited information we have about the women in Jesus' life, and seeing where it can take us. I believe my exploration, and that of the other feminists who have approached the same theme, reveals that there are astounding theological riches to be found even on the basis of the fragmentary gospel accounts. They are likely, however, to be riches of which the evangelists themselves were barely aware, for we are not just expounding the texts, but are involved in a more creative theological venture, as we address twentieth-century questions to first-century writings.

The other approach is to sketch in the blank spaces of our fragmented mosaic. Here we are engaged in a far more hypothetical venture, and it is an exercise of the imagination. We are not revealing what was, but suggesting what might have been, in the full awareness that we will never in a million years get it historically right. Here we may find we are returning to a conflationary reading of the gospels, bringing together the differing texts to make a synthesized account, not because we believe we can provide a historical reconstruction, but because we have given up on it and are looking for an imaginative reconstruction.

The reader may want to exclaim, from time to time, 'But that is not how I imagine it!' And I welcome such a response, because it contains at least the implicit recognition that we do indeed have imaginative pictures of the scriptures. Even better, people may feel challenged to form their own alternative versions. From my background in Ignatian spirituality, I do not see imagination as a rogue lurking to lead us astray, but as a powerful tool to help us engage with the texts. There is not only one way of imagining these women's stories, nor even one way for me to imagine them, for on different days I see things differently. For this book I have had to select just one possible scenario, and it makes no claim to be the correct one.

How do the six women see Jesus, once they are allowed to speak with their own voice and re-tell their memories from their own perspective? It hardly needs much of a theory of male and female differences to suggest that the stories these women would tell would be very different from the four gospels of Matthew, Mark, Luke and John which have been handed down to us.

In the imaginative way I have handled the material, the women speak more personally of Jesus than do any of the four evangelists. They are not afraid to be open about their feelings and responses. They learn more from living through events and from experiencing the way Jesus treated them than from memorizing sayings and listing miracles. The women make no attempt to hide themselves away as detached observers, nor to paste together a collection of stories handed down to them by others. They speak from the heart as participants in the gospel.

Within each woman's story I have made no attempt to give a comprehensive account of Jesus' life: Elizabeth was around only at the beginning, Photina knew him only in Samaria, and so on.

Nonetheless, if the reader takes the six accounts together, a picture of the whole life emerges.

The perspectives are different not only because they record different experiences, but also because they come from different personalities, and arise out of different states of life. The six women include the single and the married, the young and the old, the conventional and the daring, the respected and the rejected.

There are mothers and active single women; homemakers and wandering travellers; the highly-sexed and the highly-principled; the articulate and the silent; women of frustrated aspirations, and women of serene fulfilment. There are abused women and privileged women; homeless women and women with means; bereaved women and women in love; women undergoing mental torture and women singing out their joy to God. All in all, these six women, at different moments of their lives, give us such an enormously wide base of experiences that everyone should feel drawn in somewhere.

The story here is fiction. But fiction can be pregnant with truth. The notes are factual and convey information. They belong to a different order of truth. If, through one medium or the other, I am able to suggest that there was more to Jesus' relationship with women than has yet been suspected, I shall be well satisfied.

THE STORY OF
ELIZABETH

OF JUDAEA
WHO RECOGNIZED THE UNBORN CHILD

My name is Elizabeth, and I am a descendant of Aaron, the first great priest of our people. Aaron's wife was called Elisheba, so I am named after her.[1] I suppose I could be called a pious Jew, traditional in my devotion. And I have continued the priestly tradition of my family, for I married a priest: Zechariah, my husband, was also descended from Aaron.

Our son, therefore, was also priestly by descent, though he became far better known for being a prophet. Both of them are dead now. Zechariah came from the division of Abijah – one of the 24 divisions that took it in turns to attend for a week to the sabbath duties in the temple and send one of their number to enter the sanctuary.[2] Twice a year, then, he left our little hill town and went to the temple to serve.

The great sorrow of my early life was that we had no children. I had looked forward so much to being a mother. I felt so ready for it, with so much love to give. And Zechariah deserved a child: he seemed made to be a father. Month by month I hoped. For two weeks I would secretly believe that new life was blossoming within me. Then month by month I bled with sorrow, with disappointment, and with shame for whatever sin there was in me that prevented conception.[3] I came to long for an end to this exhausting

⧆

1 Luke goes out of his way to establish Elizabeth's priestly lineage (Luke 1:5), but it is a point that few people have noticed. We are given the name of Aaron's wife, so similar to Elizabeth's own name, in Exodus 6:23.

2 Scholars have reconstructed these details, following I Chronicles 24:10, 19, and 2 Chronicles 23:8.

3 It was always assumed that childlessness was the fault of the wife: it was assumed without question that it was she who was barren, not he who was infertile. But a sense of guilt for supposed inadequacy is a characteristic that has persisted in women even into the modern age.

sequence of expectation. After the menopause, they told me, when there is no hope left, then at last you can be yourself, no longer tossed on the wheel of your womb. The years dragged.

Not that I was idle as I waited. For a priestly family who make clear their faith commitment,[4] pastoral work presents itself in abundance, as those thirsty for God or for water bring themselves to your door. For a year or two I avoided any long-term commitments to others, always expecting that my time of availability would be short. Then I learned to bury myself in work, hoping that the perversity of life would bring me a child when I was least ready for it. Daughter of Aaron, I said to myself, if you have no child, then these children of God must be your children. If you have so much love to give, then give it you must: it is much needed. But in my heart I knew I was not a good mother to them, for they were my second-best children.

At last I realized I was entering the menopause, and with the ending of hope came the beginnings of a new dignity. I could start to find some serenity in our childless marriage. And now it was Zechariah's turn to serve in the temple at Jerusalem. This time he had the chief honour, fallen to him by lot, of entering the sanctuary to burn incense. It was a high point of his life, and indeed of our life together. I kissed him goodbye with pride. He would return in a little over a week.

He came back on the day expected, but not in the manner anticipated. Instead of calling out to me as he approached the house, as was his custom, he came into the house without saying a word. And I could see something was up.

'What is it?' I asked. He did not answer. There was terror in his face.[5]

'Zechariah, what is it?' I repeated. 'What has happened? Please tell me. Let me help you.' He said nothing. I waited in vain for him to begin. By now I was alarmed, for as a couple we always shared the truth between us, without secrets. Why would he not tell me? Why would he not say a word?

---

4 In Luke's picture they are both 'righteous before God, living blame-lessly according to all the commandments and regulations of the Lord' (Luke 1:6).

5 Zechariah had been terrified when he saw the angel: Luke 1:12.

But was it, after all, just fear in his face? Was there not something like joy there too? And was there perhaps some shame as well?[6]

Zechariah sat down at the table. He began to make gestures, as though asking for something. I began to understand. It was not that he would not speak, but that he could not speak. Now I was the one to be afraid. What accident had he had?

I brought him a writing tablet and a pen. He wrote 'angel'. Oh God, he had had a vision. 'What did the angel say?' I asked. He wrote 'child'. Then he wrote 'ours'. Then he wrote 'John'.

I looked at him to be sure I had not misunderstood. I asked him, 'Did the angel say we would have a child?' He nodded. 'Am I to bear you a child?' He nodded. 'Will it be a son?' He nodded. 'And are we to call him John?' He nodded. I sat down for fear of fainting. I had thought the menopause was nearly over. Now I was the one to be struck dumb – for a few moments at any rate.

After a while he picked up the pen again and wrote 'more'. 'There is something more?' He nodded. He wrote 'Numbers'. I asked, 'The book of Numbers?' He nodded. How were we to look up the book of Numbers? We would have to go to the synagogue.

I stood awkwardly in the empty synagogue as Zechariah fetched the right scroll. He unrolled to the beginning of chapter 6, and gave it to me to read,[7] pointing where I should begin and where I should end. I cleared my throat and read, and my voice echoed disconcertingly in the emptiness of the room:

> God spoke to Moses, saying: Speak to the Israelites and
> say to them: When either men or women make a special
> vow, the vow of a nazirite, to separate themselves to God,
> they shall separate themselves from wine and strong drink;
> they shall drink no wine vinegar or other vinegar, and
> shall not drink any grape juice or eat grapes, fresh or
> dried. All their days as nazirites they shall eat nothing that

6 He had been punished with dumbness for his unbelief: Luke 1:20.

7 I have attributed literacy to Elizabeth, partly for dramatic effect, and partly in harmony with my portrayal of Mary of Nazareth as literate and well-read in the scriptures: see her chapter, note 25 on p. 34.

is produced by the grapevine, not even the seeds or the skins.[8]

I looked at Zechariah expectantly. 'Are you saying he will be specially vowed to God? And he will abstain from wine as a sign of this?' He nodded. Then he fetched another scroll. It was the book of Isaiah. Again I let him point out the passage, and I read:

A voice cries out:
'In the wilderness prepare the way of the Lord,
make straight in the desert a highway for our God.
Every valley shall be lifted up,
and every mountain and hill be made low;
the uneven ground shall become level,
and the rough places a plain.
Then the glory of God shall be revealed,
and all people shall see it together.'[9]

I looked up. 'Are you saying that our son, John' (I must get used to saying these unfamiliar words), 'that our son, John, will be that voice crying in the wilderness? That he will prepare the way for God's coming?' Zechariah nodded, and fetched one more scroll, a very tiny one this time. It was the book of Malachi. I read the passage instructed, in a trembling voice:

See, I am sending my messenger to prepare the way before me, and the God whom you seek will suddenly come to his temple.[10] The messenger of the covenant in whom you

8 This passage, which is quoted by the angel Gabriel in Luke 1:15, comes from Numbers 6:1–4.

9 This passage, from Isaiah 40:3–5, is applied to John the Baptist in Luke 3:4–6, and is also quoted in part in Mark 1:3 and Matthew 3:3.

10 By using the tradition of Elizabeth and Zechariah at the beginning of his gospel, Luke is able to make the story of the Messiah begin in the temple (with the vision of the angel to Zechariah), in accordance with this prophecy from Malachi. It is interesting to note that Luke's gospel also ends in the temple: '. . . they were continually in the temple blessing God' (Luke 24:53).

delight – indeed he is coming, says the God of hosts. But who can endure the day of his coming, and who can stand when he appears? For he is like a refiner's fire and like fullers' soap; he will sit as a refiner and purifier of silver, and he will purify the descendants of Levi and refine them like gold and silver, until they present offerings to God in righteousness.[11]

It was powerful stuff, and this was to be an awe-inspiring mission. Zechariah took the scroll from me and wound on further. I read:

Lo, I will send you the prophet Elijah before the great and terrible day of the Lord comes. He will turn the hearts of parents to their children and the hearts of children to their parents.[12]

I understood. Elijah was to come to prepare the way for the Messiah. So much we were taught by the scribes, following this text of Malachi. Our son, John (I said the words to myself again), was to be the figure of Elijah. Then one question remained. Who was to be the Messiah? I said it out loud: 'Then if our son, John, is to be Elijah, who is to be the Messiah?' Zechariah shrugged. He did not know.

I did conceive. Until the third month I felt horribly, wonderfully sick. I did not want anyone to know I was pregnant in case I

11 Malachi 3:1–3. The first phrase of this prophecy is quoted of John the Baptist in Mark 1:2. The latter part of the quotation is sung in Handel's *Messiah*, as a prophecy of the coming of Christ. The purifying fire of the prophecy is evoked (with a different metaphor) by the purifying fire in the Baptist's words: 'He will baptize you with the Holy Spirit and with fire. His winnowing fork is in his hand, to clear his threshing floor and to gather the wheat into his granary; but the chaff he will burn with unquenchable fire' (Luke 3:16–17).

12 This passage comes from Malachi 4:5–6. The belief that Elijah must come again before the Messiah was open to differing interpretations. The most prevalent tradition was that John the Baptist was Elijah, but Elijah is also seen at the transfiguration, and the woman who anointed Jesus at Bethany is an Elijah figure as well: see note 15 on p. 103.

miscarried and suffered further shame. And I did not want to take any risks of miscarrying. For all these reasons I led a very secluded life for my first five months, making what excuses I could to disentangle myself from the web of pastoral commitments I had taken on. In the end there could be no doubt in others' minds about my condition – my shape gave it away. Nor could there be any doubt in my own mind, for I could feel my son, John, move within me.

I have always been a homely person, but the house began to bloom with especial joy around me, as I prepared it to be the home for a child. I sewed. I decorated. I made little toys. And in both body and soul I blossomed as I had never done before.

One day as I was preparing the vegetables for supper, I heard a woman's voice outside call my name, and immediately my son John positively leapt within me – as though with joy. A moment later a frightened, exhausted face peeped round my door. I recognized her at once – my little cousin Mary from Nazareth. Now I have always been fond of my cousin, though I rarely see her, but at this precise moment there was no one else in the world I felt more like being with. And she looked in so much need.

How I knew it I do not understand, but somehow at that moment I realized exactly what had happened to her. She too was pregnant – just – and she was in disgrace. Since I myself had been in disgrace for so much of my own life – for exactly the opposite reason, for *not* being pregnant – I felt deeply for her. But that was only the half of what I understood. For I also knew that the prophet within me had recognized the embryo within her. She was bearing the Messiah.

I rose and clasped her hands with joy and cried out with delight, and with an inspiration that seemed to come from God, 'Mary, Mary. What a blessed woman you are, among all women,[13] and what a blessed child that is that you are carrying. And how lucky I am to have you visit me in your condition: what

13 When Elizabeth greets Mary as 'blessed among women', she is echoing the phrase used of two very brave women in the Old Testament, who destroyed the power of enemy leaders by assassinating them – Jael (Judges 5:24) and Judith (Judith 13:18; some bibles put Judith in the Apocrypha). This prepares the way for Mary's Magnificat, which praises God for overthrowing those in power.

have I done to deserve a visit from the mother of the Messiah?'[14] Do you know, my own child jumped for joy inside me when he heard your voice? Bless you, Mary, for believing the promise of God.'[15]

And Mary cried from relief and happiness, and her words bubbled out as the tears did, as though for the first time she was able to let herself be happy about her condition. I had never known her so vocal. She thanked God and praised God in the terms so familiar to our ancestors,[16] and yet she was applying the language

14 Jane Schaberg writes: 'Elizabeth makes the first and only Christological confession by a woman in this gospel: "Why has this happened to me, that the mother of my Lord comes to me?" (1:43). "Lord" is for Luke here and in many other places a Christian title for Jesus, affirming his transcendent dominion' (*Women's Bible Commentary*, eds Carol A. Newsom and Sharon H. Ringe, SPCK, 1992, pp. 282–3). J. Massyngbaerde Ford explains further: 'This title was used of God and of important persons, such as kings and owners of slaves' (*My Enemy Is My Guest: Jesus and Violence in Luke*, Orbis, 1984, p. 20).

15 If Mary has been likened to Judith a moment earlier, there is an important contrast at this point in the kind of action the two women undertook to fulfil God's purposes. In Judith, God 'foiled them by the hand of a woman', because Judith had cut off the head of the Assyrian leader, Holofernes. (The quote comes from Judith's song of praise, which parallels Mary's Magnificat.) In Mary, God 'has done great things' (v. 49) and 'brought down the powerful' (v. 52), simply because Mary had 'believed that there would be a fulfilment of what was spoken to her'. (See also note 4 on the *fiat* on p. 23.)

16 Mary's psalm of praise (Luke 1:47–55), known as the Magnificat from its first word in Latin, is based largely on the song of Hannah in 1 Samuel 2:1–10. Other echoes come from all over the Old Testament, for example, Exodus 6:6, Psalms 35:9, 89:13, 99:3–5, 118:28. Indeed the Magnificat has been described as a mosaic of Old Testament allusions.

In one or two old Latin manuscripts, and in quotations of this passage by Irenaeus (c. AD 180), the Magnificat is said by Elizabeth (whose position as a middle-aged woman expecting her first baby is parallel to that of Hannah). But this is very much a minority reading, for the overwhelming textual evidence puts it in the mouth of Mary.

of the scriptures to her own situation, and finding out the truth of God's word for today.[17]

She said she was just a humble, ordinary girl who had received this unexpected and undeserved favour. She said everyone would call her blessed from now on, once they had seen what a great thing God had done for her. God is holy, she said, holy, holy, and merciful and mighty. And she said that what had been done in her was just the way God had always acted in the past – scattering the proud, unseating the powerful, and dismissing the wealthy, while lifting up the simple people and feeding the hungry with unexpected abundance. She said that what was done today was a fulfilment of the promise God made to our ancestors. Sarah had been given the child of the promise in her old age. And the two of us were given children of salvation today, when for our various reasons we both thought pregnancy was impossible. It was the same promise as that entrusted to Sarah, she said, the same continuing story of salvation for God's people.

As Mary was pouring all this out, I could see behind her that Zechariah had come into the house. He stopped at the door and listened, and maybe he too understood, though he could not say so. When Mary had finished I told her she must stay with us just as long as she could. And then Zechariah made his presence known and made signs of agreement.

It was good in those weeks to have someone to talk to, rather than conducting monologues with Zechariah all the time; good to share a pregnancy, cherishing our bodies and growing together; and most of all good to be in constant company with the mother of the Messiah, who was so blessed with understanding, and whose child was here with us (even if hidden), saturating our house with peace. I always felt close to Jesus in later years, even though I hardly met him as an adult, because I had had such a strong sense of his presence under our own roof.

In the end Mary stayed with us three months, just up until John's birth. And then, having glimpsed the first child of the promise, she felt she must go back home and face the music. She

∞

17 This is the method of liberation theology – to read the scriptures in the context of present reality, and find in them a contemporary message.

missed her boyfriend, who had told her he could no longer marry her, and she wanted to attempt a reconciliation with him.[18]

There was wild joy in my family when our child was born, and relatives and friends were in the house morn and night. They were all around for the circumcision, on the eighth day. The men performing the rite were just about to name him Zechariah after his father – they did not even have the courtesy to ask me, they just thought they knew best – but I butted in: 'No', I said, 'he is to be called John.' They treated me like a fool, who had no right to say what my own son's name was. 'None of your relatives has that name', they told me, as though I did not know. 'It does not matter', I said firmly, 'he is to be named John.' They still would not accept it, and said they would have to ask Zechariah. Now he still could not speak, so we had this absurd spectacle of Zechariah being given a writing tablet and pen so he could write down what I had already told them. 'His name is John', he wrote. They were amazed.

But a moment later they were still more amazed, for he began to speak. It was as though that little act of fidelity to God had broken through the paralysis brought by fear, and had loosed his tongue. Men had tried to argue him out of naming our child according to the message of the angel, and he had resisted, and insisted, and found his liberation in it.[19]

To say he began to speak is something of an understatement, for just as Mary had poured out her praises, magnifying God, so did Zechariah now he had at last broken through the barrier of dumbness. He blessed God for looking favourably on our people, and for bringing us a saviour from David's family. (Now by this he meant Mary's baby, for Mary's boyfriend was descended from

18 Betrothal was a more serious and settled arrangement than modern engagement, so a reconciliation would be more like healing a marriage rift.

19 Luke says '. . . all these things were talked about throughout the entire hill country of Judaea' (Luke 1:65), which is often taken as an indication that Luke is incorporating an oral tradition current in the Judaean churches, rather than making the whole story up himself, as has sometimes been suggested.

David.) He recalled the prophecies – just as he had done to me, that day when he had got me to look them up. And especially he remembered the ones that said we would be saved from our enemies and from all those who hate us, so that we could serve God without fear, in a holy and just way, all through our lives. It is the same promise that God had always made, he declared (and this was what Mary had said, too). It is the same oath that God had made back in the days of Sarah and Abraham, and in the days of Moses and my ancestor Aaron. And then he turned to our son John and gave him his big finger to grasp in the baby's tiny hand, and he said, 'You're going to be a great prophet of God, aren't you, little one? You're going to prepare the way for the Messiah, and teach people to be sorry for their sins, aren't you?' And his new voice sang with an unfamiliar poetic passion as he told us all, 'By God's tender mercy, the dawn will break on us from the heavens, and the light will pour down on those who are crouching in the darkness and in the shadow of death, and by that light we will pick our path, until we walk in the way of peace.'[20]

Our son John grew up. He was a strong lad, and a very spiritual person, but that was about the limit of his resemblance to his parents. We had always been a reasonably traditional couple, and by now of course we were elderly as well. John by contrast was a wild young thing. He looked a scruff, and he had some pretty eccentric habits. He lived alone in the desert. He ate locusts and wild honey. He would not touch alcohol. And he dressed in a camel skin. None of this, however, was much of a surprise to us, since we had been warned he would be a prophet. Elijah, after all, had done much the same. He dressed in animal skins, and lived a solitary life east of Jordan, where he was fed by the ravens.[21]

Priests and prophets are really quite different personalities, and have quite different tasks to fulfil in the service of God. I was the daughter of the great priest, Aaron, and Zechariah was priestly too: we hallowed and preserved the traditional cult, by which most

---

20 Zechariah's hymn of praise (Luke 1:68–79) is customarily known as the Benedictus (from its first word in Latin).

21 We know this from 1 Kings 17:3–7 and 2 Kings 1:8.

people, most of the time, were able to find their comfort in God. John was prophetic: he challenged and disturbed the habitual religious ways. But we were wonderfully proud of him. We knew he was right, and we learned a lot from him.

The time came for Zechariah to leave this world. You will have gathered that we were a very close couple, bound together by our faith and love of God. I could never have married anyone who did not share that most important part of my life. All our lives we had shared everything and supported each other in everything – the service of God, the grief of childlessness, the labour of bringing up a very lively little boy when we were past our more energetic years, the challenge of seeing our precious son go off to lead his strange life in isolation. I could not imagine how I would live without Zechariah at my side to share the joys and struggles and sorrows. I had never lived alone.

I yearned for Zechariah and knew an old widow's life was basically one of waiting for death. The extra bodily strength that we women have, that keeps us in life and health for years after our husbands have died, can be a terrible burden. Why can we not live to the full and then die promptly, as men do? Why these spun out years of solitary life as our bodies slowly crack? My friends said, 'Surely John will come back, now you are alone. Hopefully he will have enough sense of duty to know his place is with his mother in her widowhood.' They did not make it easy for me. John did not come back. God was preparing him in the desert to be a prophet. That was more important than looking after his old mum. At least I knew that, and was free from the burden of disappointed expectation.

Nor were my last years tranquil. John began to be famous. That was not the end, of course, it was only a prelude to the awfulness of the end. But for a while I began to be treated as something of a celebrity myself, for being the mother of the prophet. Fame is a strange creature, the way it springs up suddenly, after you have been doing the same thing for years without anyone noticing. By the time John was 30 he had been living in the wilderness for years, but people rather suddenly began to discover him as though he had not been there before. They sensed a tremendous spiritual attraction in him, and would go out into the desert just to hear him talk about God. He told them bluntly to repent of their sins, and, if they did, he baptized them with water as a sign of their resolution to change and of God's cleansing of their past.

More and more people went out to him. Crowds and crowds.

Sometimes he was quite rude to them, calling them 'children of vipers'.[22] They loved it. He would launch an attack on anyone – priests and politicians above all. He even condemned the tetrarch, Herod Antipas, for sexual immorality.[23] I had to hold my breath sometimes, fighting down my impulse to urge him to be careful. Daughter of Aaron, I said to myself, do not stand in the path of God. Remember that John's work is to flatten mountains and to fill in the valleys.[24] It is no delicate business. It needs the brawn of an ox.

By now John was hugely, hugely famous, and was known throughout the country as the Baptist. Everyone I knew of had been baptized by him, unless they were lawyers or Pharisees – the two groups who were still suspicious.[25] I went out myself from time to time to hear him: it was the only chance I got to see my son. And I too asked to be baptized, for I wanted to prepare myself to meet God.

People began to say John was the Messiah, and he had to tell them very firmly that he was not. He said, 'So much am I not the Messiah that I am not even worthy to untie the thong of his sandals.'[26] Considering that the Messiah was his own cousin you can see what a sense of his own unworthiness our son John had. It was not just others who were told to repent: he knew he was a sinner just as they were. 'But', he continued, 'the Messiah *is*

22 This is said to Pharisees and Sadducees in Matthew 3:7, but to the crowds in Luke 3:7.

23 Herod had married Herodias, who was the wife of his brother Philip, and John condemned the marriage as unlawful (Matthew 14:3–4, Mark 6:17–18 and Luke 3:19).

24 This is a quotation from the prophecy of Isaiah 40:4: see above.

25 Luke 7:29–30 tells us that these two groups refused to be baptized by John, while everyone else in the crowd listening to Jesus had submitted to his baptism.

26 This is one of the best attested sayings in the New Testament, occurring in five books: Matthew 3:11, Mark 1:7, Luke 3:16, John 1:27, Acts 13:25.

coming. You may think that what you are getting from me is powerful stuff, but that is nothing to what is on its way. I baptized you with water, but the Messiah will baptize you with the Spirit of God and with fire. The wind of the Spirit[27] will blow apart the chaff from the wheat. The wheat will be gathered and stored safely in barns. But the chaff will be burned up in a fire that will never go out.'

This was the scene into which Mary's son erupted. John recognized him as immediately as he had done as a babe in my womb, leaping for joy. 'That's the one!' he cried, but it took a few months for the crowds to follow John's pointing finger.[28] When they began to do so, the stragglers asked John if he minded being displaced by Jesus. What a silly question. What did they think John was doing, if not preparing the way for Jesus? Yet it became a huge talking point – whether John or Jesus was pulling bigger crowds – as though they were rivals.[29]

This imaginary rivalry was short-lived, for John was arrested and imprisoned. It was his attack on Herod's sexual conduct that did it, for Herod had married Herodias, who was his brother's wife, and John was proclaiming to all the crowds that this was unlawful. I was told of the arrest on the evening it happened, because some friends had gone out to see him in the desert and came back with the news that he was no longer there. They broke it to me gently and, though I was obviously shaken, I was also proud that he was suffering for his faith. I have to admit I was also confident he would be released. 'Now the Messiah has come', I told them, 'we need have no more fear. Salvation is right at hand.' How wrong I was in thinking that meant John would be freed. It took most of us a long time to understand what sort of Messiah had come in Jesus.

27 'Spirit' and 'wind' are the same word in the Greek – pneuma. See Matthew 3:11–12, Luke 3:15–17. See also note 36 on p. 21 below.

28 In Christian art, John is habitually shown (even as a baby) pointing at Jesus. This comes from the fourth gospel, where John exclaims, 'Look, there is the Lamb of God!' (John 1:36), and it is principally John's gospel that I am following at this juncture.

29 The supposed rivalry is reported in John 4:1–3.

I could not often obtain access to John in prison, though as the only close family member, and a 'harmless' old woman,[30] I was the only person who could be sure to gain access eventually. It is humiliating for any woman to go to jail and beg permission to see a prisoner. But for the wife of a priest it is perhaps especially hard, for though I had lived through my years of childless disgrace I was not used to being treated as the mother of a criminal. What is more, I was old now and slow of foot, and the journey was exhausting for me. They are right who say that the women relatives of prisoners suffer as much as those inside, for they know the sufferings of their menfolk, and can do nothing to help.

I have keenly painful memories of one visit. He was thin, but I was used to that. He was unkempt, but I was used to that too. What I was not used to was seeing his spirit so low. The guards were trying to undermine his beliefs, that was one problem, and their half-lies were mingling with accounts that were coming in from outside, and John did not know what to think. He had heard that Jesus did not fast, but on the contrary led an undisciplined life of self-indulgence, feasting and drinking.[31] I tried to defend Jesus. He said, 'Stop making excuses, just tell me if it is true.' I could not deny that he liked to eat and drink well. Now this was something most undermining to John, whose entire spirituality had always been founded on asceticism – living in the desert with no money and surviving on the odd locust. It was a good preparation for prison life, for he felt the deprivations and solitude, the hunger and insults, less than the others, but it was not a good preparation for understanding the lifestyle of Jesus.

I remember John grasping me by the arm with doubt and fear in his wild eyes, and begging me to ask Jesus if he was really the

30 When Christian feminists want to reassert the wisdom and dignity of old women, they sometimes use the term 'crone' to describe them. 'Crones' are customarily passed over and dismissed as useless, but they have unappreciated gifts. See Barbara G. Walker, *The Crone: Woman of Age, Wisdom and Power* (HarperCollins, 1985).

31 We can deduce this, not only from Matthew 9:14 and 11:18–19, but also from the number of dinners recorded in the gospels.

Messiah, or if we were to wait for another.[32] 'I'm sure he's the Messiah', I told him, trying to shore up my faith as well as his, but that was not good enough. 'No, mother', he said, 'you must ask.' 'But', I objected, 'Jesus is a long way off. When you were arrested he moved straightaway out of range. Ever since you were put in prison he has been in Galilee.[33] It is too far for me to travel.' 'Then you must send my friends. Promise to send someone. Promise to bring back the news as soon as ever you can.' I remember thinking that he must believe in Jesus deep down or he would not set such store by his answer. And yet I could not get out of my mind afterwards the desperation in his face and voice. I knew that in the prison there was nothing to take his mind off his worries, and he would sit and brood. There was no comfort there but prayer, and when prayer fails and faith wavers, then where do you look?

The answer, when it came, was an oblique one. I was not allowed another visit so close to the last one, so we sent in a letter. We knew it would be censored, so we never quite knew if he had got the message until my next visit some weeks later. The message was that Jesus had replied, 'Go and tell John what you hear and see: the blind receive their sight, the lame walk, the lepers are cleansed, the deaf hear, the dead are raised, and the poor have good news brought to them. And blessed is anyone who takes no offence at me.' It was only after we had sent in the letter that we heard from others that Jesus had been praising John to the skies. He had said he was 'a prophet, and more than a prophet'. He had said he was 'Elijah, who was to come'. And he had said solemnly that 'among those born of women there has been no one greater than John the Baptist'. As the woman of whom John was born that made me feel very special. I longed for my next visit, when I could pass that news on to John himself to lift his spirits.

When I next saw him I was much relieved to find him more at peace. I had been anxious that he was worrying, while in fact his mind had found some rest. I told him on this occasion that I could not believe he would be much longer in prison, because public opinion was so strongly united in his favour. He told me that

∽∾

32 This incident (without any mention of Elizabeth's involvement) is recorded in Matthew 11:2–14 and Luke 7:22–28.

33 We know this from Matthew 4:12 and Mark 1:14.

what happened was now up to God: his work was over, and he was ready to accept whatever came to him. But release he admitted was quite possible, because he could confirm that Herod seemed well disposed towards him. They had had several sessions together, when curiosity had driven Herod to hear this famous holy man. And he had seemed to receive what he had heard with favour,[34] even though John was not softening his tune to play safe with him. Herod was vicious and not to be trusted an inch,[35] and yet he was not immune, any more than anyone else was, to John's extraordinary charism. In fact John now suspected that the only reason he was still detained in prison was so that Herod could keep him there to listen to when he chose. For the man who had everything he wanted, and every possible adviser and expert, a pet prophet was the ultimate designer luxury.

I never saw John again alive. The news of his beheading was like an axe blow in my own body. I expect you know what happened. Herod had a banquet on his birthday, and the daughter of Herodias danced for him, which gave him great pleasure. Herod was drunk and swore he would give her any gift she requested. She consulted with her mother, who wanted to get rid of John because he had denounced her relationship with Herod. She told her daughter what to ask for. This is not easy for me to say. She asked for John's head. Sit down before I tell you this: they carried it into the banquet on a plate.

His friends brought out the body to where I was waiting with a little group at a tomb. So the last time I saw John he had no head. But a mother does not need a head to know when she is looking at the body of her child.

It left me dead, even as I lived. Every night I thought I would not wake again, for I had no heart left and no spirit either. I did not know how my lungs could find the energy to go on breathing,

34 'Herod feared John, knowing that he was a righteous and holy man, and he protected him. When he heard him he was greatly perplexed; and yet he liked to listen to him' (Mark 6:20). The story of the dance and John's beheading follows on.

35 Later Jesus is warned that Herod wants to kill him, and he calls him a 'fox' (Luke 13:31–32). See also Mark 8:15, where Jesus warns his disciples to beware of the yeast of Herod.

in and out.[36] But my body perversely refused to stop. They told me Jesus was devastated.[37] So he should be, I thought. What hope was there for the Messiah now? How long till he too was killed?

It was not long, and when it came it came with a savagery that made me think my son John was blessed to go the way he did. And yet it was through that most cruel murder that I found my peace at last.

Their deaths were not pointless, nor were they the end of our hopes, for through their deaths the people have been transformed. John is now revered as a martyr, whose death, like his life, led the way for the Messiah. Then as Jesus joined John in death, so John was able to be lifted up by Jesus in the burst of jubilant freedom that followed. What a difference there is between being the mother of an executed criminal and being the mother of an exemplary martyr! The liberation we have received through these deaths is different from what we expected. But it is not lesser. It is greater.

I am still waiting to die, but now I wait with pride and with a joyful longing to be with my husband and son and cousin, who have passed not from life to death, but rather from this world of death to the promised land of limitless life.

36 Because the same word is used for 'breath' and for 'spirit', not only in Greek (*pneuma*) but also in Hebrew (*ruah*), the breath in a body is taken in a particularly literal way as the gift of God's Spirit. God breathes life into a body ('I will . . . put breath/spirit in you, and you shall live', Ezekiel 37:6), or takes away the breath of life ('When you take away their breath/spirit, they die and return to their dust', Psalm 104:29).

37 When Jesus heard of John's death, 'he withdrew from there in a boat to a desert place by himself' (Matthew 14:13).

THE STORY OF
M A R Y

My name is Mary of Nazareth, and I am the mother of Jesus. People have called me by a lot of extravagant titles,[1] but I think you should know I am a very ordinary woman.

You came to know Jesus later, after he became a controversial public figure. But I knew him before anyone else in the world. I knew him from the first, tiny, tappings of his feet in my womb, just about the time that my pregnancy was beginning to show at around three months. From then on I felt in communion with him, and day by day I felt our relationship growing stronger.

I had very mixed feelings about the pregnancy. I do not want to say much about it now, except that it was not exactly planned and it took me totally by surprise.[2] From surprise I felt joy and privilege – that amazing feeling that I had created another human being of unique quality. Just as my body was stretching and growing and making something new, so my soul felt it was stretching out and growing into the glory of God and making a new song of

1 Mary of Nazareth's titles include Blessed Virgin Mary, Mother of God (see note 10 on p. 27), the Immaculate Conception (defined by Pope Pius IX in 1854), Our Lady, Queen of Heaven, Co-Redeemer, Mary Immaculate, Star of the Sea, Ark of the Covenant, Tower of David, Gate of Heaven, Refuge of Sinners, Mother of Mercy, Help of Christians, Queen of Peace, etc.

2 The traditions recorded in Matthew and Luke speak of Mary conceiving by the power of the Holy Spirit. According to Luke, the news that she was to conceive was brought to her by the angel Gabriel while she was still a virgin. Luke 3:23 and Matthew 1:18–19 indicate that the child was not Joseph's.

The ancient tradition of the Church has interpreted these texts as meaning that Jesus had no human father, and this was a virginal conception. (See also note 31 on p. 37 on Mary's virginity.)

In an original interpretation, Jane Schaberg suggests that Mary

praise for the Creator.³ In my excitement I pledged myself to the new direction my life was going to take, praying, 'Let your will be done in me. I will serve you in whatever way you want.'⁴ I thanked God for choosing someone as ordinary as me to have such a special child (and I already had a pretty good idea of just how

may have been the victim of rape, and that behind the two gospel accounts lies a tradition of Jesus' illegitimacy, which has been sensitively presented with a positive, religious interpretation. 'Neither evangelist intends to deny the tradition of Jesus' illegitimacy. If each were asked about it, he would reply, "Yes, I do intend to hand down this tradition. Yes . . . but" ' (*The Illegitimacy of Jesus*, Harper and Row, 1987). She says: 'Mary is a woman who has access to the sacred outside the patriarchal family and its control. The illegitimate conception turns out to be grace not disgrace, order within disorder. On the basis of belief in the Holy Spirit who empowers the conception of Jesus and his resurrection, and who creates and elects all, a community is believed possible' (p. 199).

   If Mary was the victim of sexual violence, then the divine promise is of God's transforming creative power, in bringing salvation out of evil. 'In the case of Jesus, what is overcome is his mother's deeper humiliation, the violation of a betrothed virgin. In this context, Mary's canticle, the Magnificat, is powerfully appropriate' (*Women's Bible Commentary*, p. 284). Schaberg explains the Lucan text: 'In the dialogue between Gabriel and Mary, Gabriel's response (1:34) is not an explanation of how the pregnancy is to come about but is a statement of reassurance, urging trust. The verbs "come upon" and "overshadow" promise empowerment and protection (cf. Acts 1:8; Luke 9:34). These verbs have no sexual or creative connotations. Mary's question "How?" is sidestepped and remains unanswered.'

3 These are feelings expressed in Mary's psalm of praise, known as the Magnificat from its first word in Latin. 'My soul magnifies the Lord, and my spirit rejoices in God my Saviour, for he has looked with favour on the lowliness of his servant . . .' (Luke 1:47–48).

4 These were Mary's words to Gabriel: 'Here am I, the servant [or slave] of God; let it be with me according to your word' (Luke 1:38). I have simply re-translated, and reversed the order of the clauses, and have

special he was going to be). I might have known in theory that God typically favours the ordinary people, and passes by the people who think they are important, because they have money or rank or political power;[5] but in practice I found it hard to believe it was

treated this as Mary's characteristic prayer, to be repeated many times in her life. Traditionally the attitude of this prayer, summed up in the single Latin word, *fiat*, 'let it be', is taken to express the heart of Mary's spirituality and the essence of her prayerful example to the Christian.

The *fiat* has been damaging to women in their spirituality when it has been taken to imply an attitude of female submission rather than of human submission. In this way a misconstrued *fiat* approach has encouraged women to continue to submit to discrimination from society and to oppression or even violence from men. Humility and silence are then taken as virtues, and any attempt to right the injustice or emerge from the oppression is taken as a sign of stridency. But this is an idolatrous distortion of the spirituality of the *fiat*, because submission to God's will has been replaced by submission to men's will. Any attempt to promote Mary as more of a model for women than for men should therefore be treated with great suspicion.

St Bernard attached great importance to Mary's reply to Gabriel. Without such an expression of explicit consent, he implies, Mary would not have conceived and humanity would still be awaiting its salvation. This emphasis is particularly interesting today, when there is such a development of the idea that women have the right to control their fertility and to make their own choices about whether to bear a child. (Of course, very different considerations apply in the case of choosing to terminate pregnancy from those which apply in the case of choosing to avoid pregnancy.) Here is what Bernard said:

'The angel is waiting for your answer: it is time for him to return to God who sent him. We too are waiting, O Lady, for the word of pity, even we who are overwhelmed in wretchedness by the sentence of damnation. . . . Open, O Blessed Virgin, your heart to faith; open your lips to speak; open your bosom to your Maker. Behold! the Desired of all nations is outside, knocking at your door. Oh! if by your delay he should pass by. . . . Open by your word. And Mary said: "Behold the handmaid of the Lord: be it done to me according to your word" ' (*Homilies*, 4).

5 This reversal of worldly fortune is the central insight of Mary's Magnificat:

happening to someone quite as ordinary as me.[6] All the ordinary things of my life – my ordinary house, my ordinary possessions, my ordinary clothes, my ordinary activities – seemed touched by love because they had been chosen by God as a home for Jesus.

But after the initial burst of joy I felt anxiety, fear and grief, as the reality of the situation bore in on me. I told my fiancé

'He has brought down the powerful from their thrones,
and lifted up the lowly;
he has filled the hungry with good things,
and sent the rich away empty.' (Luke 1:52–53)

6   The identification of Mary with the ordinary and lowly people of the world has been a mark of much popular devotion, as Catholics of different nations claim her as their own. For example, the devotion of Our Lady of Guadalupe rests on a sixteenth-century vision of a Mexican Indian, who believed he saw Mary as an Indian woman, with brown skin. The abundance of 'Our Lady of . . .' titles, which are distasteful to many, is favourably interpreted by others as an expression of incarnational belief, in the sense that God is seen to make a dwelling place among all the humble peoples of the world.

However, the ordinariness of Mary has also been misused for more sinister purposes, to bolster up male fantasies about the ideal of the simple, uneducated, unambitious, contented woman who finds all her fulfilment in being a wife and mother. Martin Luther, for example, writes of Mary the mother of Jesus: 'Behold how completely she traces all to God, lays claim to no works, no honour, no fame. . . . She seeks not any glory, but goes about her usual household duties, milking the cows, cooking the meals, washing pots and kettles, sweeping out the rooms, . . . as though she cared nothing for such great gifts and graces. She was esteemed among other women and her neighbours no more highly than before, nor desired to be, but remained a poor townswoman, one of the great multitude. Oh, how simple and pure a heart was hers, how strange a soul was this! What great things are hidden here under this lowly exterior! How many came in contact with her, talked, and ate, and drank with her, who perhaps counted her but a common, poor, and simple village maiden' (Commentary on the *Magnificat, Luther's Works*, vol. 21, ed. Jaroslav Pelikan, St Louis, 1956, pp. 326, 329. For this extract, and for that from St Bernard in note 4, I am indebted to Eamon Duffy's *What Catholics Believe About Mary*, Catholic Truth Society, 1989.)

straightaway, and I have never known him so hurt. The worst was knowing that it was I who had hurt him. Joseph did not understand. Even so, he tried to behave in a way that would cause me the minimum of hurt and shame. Instead of denouncing me in public and so giving some vent to his feelings, he bottled them up and told me he would break off the engagement privately.[7] I felt a terrible hole inside: for the sake of a son I had never seen I was to lose the only man I had ever loved. You see what I mean about mixed feelings about the pregnancy? I almost hated the child within me for taking Joseph away from me. But I kept on praying to God, 'Let your will be done in me. I will serve you in whatever way you want', even though I spent most of the day in tears. I needed support, but with Joseph alienated from me there did not seem anyone to turn to except God. My mother is very understanding,[8] but I was afraid of the brave front my parents would put on – loving and supporting without understanding. I did not know how I would tell them. But how long could I hide it? In the end, I wrote them a note, and ran away.

I ran to my cousin's house – a two-day journey away in the hills of Judaea. I had not seen her since I was a child, and I hoped no one would suspect I had gone there. She was some 25 years older than me, and was a descendant of the great priest Aaron. She

No doubt comparable passages can be found in an abundance of Catholic writers, but this is such a good example of what infuriates many modern women that I have thought it worth quoting. It is difficult to imagine a man being praised so effusively for leading such humble, lowly life. It is to counteract such an attitude to women that I have balanced Mary's ordinariness and humility with a presentation of her as the more educated partner in the marriage, and indeed as an original theologian of decisive importance for the development of Christian thought (see the end of the chapter).

7 'Joseph, being a righteous man and unwilling to expose her to public disgrace, planned to dismiss her quietly' (Matthew 1:19). Betrothal was a more serious and settled arrangement than modern engagement, so this was more like a divorce than a broken engagement would be today.

8 By tradition, Mary's mother was called Anna (sometimes translated Anne), and her father was called Joachim.

was also married to a priest of the temple at Jerusalem.[9] Because they had no children I hoped she might have room to take me in for a while, to give me a chance to adjust to the shock of my pregnancy in some privacy, before it became public knowledge. I was very afraid on the way, because I did not know how she would react. If she took me in, she would be in disgrace for having an unmarried mother-to-be in her household. If she did not, she would be in disgrace for turning away a relative in need. I hated the thought of turning up without warning, and forcing this dilemma on her, especially since I knew what a good and kind person she was and I did not want to exploit her generosity. But I could not think of anything else to do, or anywhere else to go.

I walked up the hill to her house, dusty, tired, hungry and, most of all, frightened of what I had to tell her. As I came to the threshold I called out weakly, 'Elizabeth?', and then cautiously pushed open the door. Elizabeth was sitting in a chair in the corner, peeling vegetables – a picture of serenity and homeliness, and I saw that for the first time in her life she was quite obviously pregnant herself. It was almost strange to see that big tummy beneath that worn and lined face, strange to think of Elizabeth, of all people, as a mother-to-be. She sat there with a pensive look on her face and one hand lightly resting on her tummy, which even I could see was heaving about as the child changed position.

Then she got up hurriedly, if somewhat clumsily, looking so happy to see me that the tears began to roll down my dusty face. She came and shook me heartily by both hands and beamed with satisfaction. 'You are the luckiest woman in the world', she told me, 'and what a wonderful child you are carrying.[10] How come I'm

---

9 If Elizabeth and Zechariah, her husband, were both from the priestly tribe, then their relationship to Mary and Joseph, who both came from the tribe of David, could not have been all that close. Nonetheless, Luke 1:36 says Mary and Elizabeth were relatives.

10 Probably the most important title given to Mary is *theotokos*, which is usually translated 'Mother of God', but more accurately means 'God-bearer'. In other words, it does not imply that Mary somehow generated the divine nature from within herself, but simply that the

so privileged as to have you visit me at such a moment? As soon as I heard your voice the child inside me jumped for joy.'[11] And then my floodgates really opened, for she knew and she understood.

Nothing gave me strength like that visit did. We were more like sisters than cousins, despite our age difference. Elizabeth enabled me to enjoy my pregnancy, to be proud of my child and wholeheartedly grateful for him. I was so happy for her, and she was so happy for me, and our happiness reflected off each other and grew and grew, just as our babies did. I stayed there three months – just long enough to see my little cousin born, who was also a boy.[12] Without that long and peaceful summer in which we ate all the right foods and did all the right exercises and measured our expanding girths together, I would never have had the courage to go back home and face up to my friends and relations again. But I think Elizabeth has already told you about the visit.

While I was away Joseph changed his mind once again about

child that she was carrying was divine, even in her womb. The Council of Ephesus in 431 declared that Mary was *theotokos* (Latin, *deipara*), in the following formulation: 'One and the same is the eternal Son of the Father and the Son of the Virgin Mary. She may therefore rightly be called *Theotokos*.' The *theotokos* doctrine became symbolically important for its Christological implications, that Jesus was truly God and truly human. The title of *theotokos* is particularly prominent in Orthodox devotion. (For a fuller discussion of the controversy leading up to the definition at Ephesus see Mary T. Malone, *Who Is My Mother?* Wm C. Brown Co., Iowa, 1984, pp. 32–40, and Aloys Grillmeier, *Christ in Christian Tradition*, vol. 1, John Knox Press, Atlanta, GA/Mowbray, London and Oxford, 1975, pp. 443–84, 559–68.)

11 Her words, from Luke 1:42–44, are recalled in the 'Hail Mary' prayer: '. . . Blessed art thou among women, and blessed is the fruit of thy womb, Jesus.'

12 Luke leaves it ambiguous whether Mary left just before or just after the birth. She goes to visit after the angel has told her Elizabeth is in the sixth month of pregnancy (Luke 1:36), and she stays about three months (Luke 1.56). Mary's departure is mentioned before the story is told of John's birth (in verses 57ff.), but this does not necessarily imply chronological sequence.

our marriage. Someone apparently told him[13] I had not been unfaithful to him as he thought, and helped him to see that this child would be a wonderful gift. And instead of feeling excluded from the relationship by my carrying a child that was not his own, he began to think about the difficulties we would face without him: I would be an unmarried mother; the baby would be a bastard. By the time I returned, Joseph was desperate to make things up with me, to adopt the baby as his own, and to push ahead with the marriage at the earliest possible date. He told me our marriage would bring him two precious people instead of one.

Nothing in my life, however, has worked out quite the way I hoped. Just as I was coming up to term, we were sent to the other end of the country for a census by the Romans – nobody's favourite people. And so I travelled to Bethlehem,[14] nine months pregnant, without a doctor, without a midwife, without so much as a booking in a hotel. It was mad. There was no proper provision for receiving all the visitors, and no allowance for special cases needing urgent accommodation. All the hotels were full, and we were still looking for somewhere to stay when I went into labour.

Joseph rushed around, begging people for a bed for me, asking for an emergency midwife, and yet trying not to leave me on my own for too long. Things were chaotic and time was short: we never found a midwife, and when Joseph still could not find a bed

<hr>

13 According to Matthew 1:20, 'an angel of the Lord appeared to him in a dream'.

14 Luke and Matthew give different explanations of how Jesus of Nazareth came to be born in Bethlehem. An explanation is needed because Nazareth is in Galilee, the northern part of the country, and Bethlehem is in the south, but a Bethlehem birth was necessary to fulfil the prophecies. According to Matthew, the family appeared to have originated in Judaea but moved to Galilee after their stay in Egypt, to avoid Herod's son Archelaus (Matthew 2:22). Luke's explanation, by contrast – and this has become the overwhelming devotional tradition of the Church – is that the family originally came from Nazareth, but was temporarily in Bethlehem for a census ordered by the Emperor Augustus. This is the tradition I have followed here, not because it is necessarily more likely to be the true explanation, but because there is no particular gain in departing from such an entrenched and well-loved story.

I decided I could go no further. The gaps between contractions were not long enough for me to walk the streets a moment longer. I staggered into the nearest stable, lay down on the straw and refused to move.

I think Joseph felt bad because he had not found a room, and embarrassed because we were in someone else's stable, but he held my hand and tried to give me confidence through the labour pains,[15] though it was the first time for him as it was for me. I had no idea labour would hurt so much. I used to tell Jesus years later that when you are having a baby you do not think anything can ever make up for the pain; and yet when the baby was born I was so filled with joy that I forgot the hurt.[16]

Every mother thinks her baby is the best in the world, but I knew mine was. It was as though the stars were singing that night, and the stable – that I would normally think was dirty and smelly with its steaming patches of manure – became like a palace. The starlight shone through the gaps in the wood, the breathing of the animals was like a soothing lullaby, and there was a manger there against the wall that would keep the baby safe from being trampled underfoot, like a little cot made just for him. Joseph wrapped up this tiny baby boy, perfectly formed, in a piece of white cloth, and they both fell asleep exhausted. I did not sleep. I was too excited. I kept on getting up to look at my baby, and from

15 One tradition, which has not been followed in this account, says that Mary gave birth without labour pains and without the breaking of the hymen. For example the fifth-century preacher Proclus, from the Alexandrian theological tradition, said: 'Emmanuel has opened the gates of nature because he was man, but he did not break the seals of virginity because he was God. As Ezekiel the prophet said, "This gate will be kept shut. No one will open it or go through it, since Yahweh, the God of Israel, has been through it. And so, it must be kept shut." ' (Quoted in Hilda Graef, *Mary: a History of Doctrine and Devotion*, Sheed and Ward, New York, 1963, p. 104.)

16 Jesus' saying, from John 16:21, might have been based on information first given him by his mother: 'When a woman is in labour, she has pain, because her hour has come. But when her child is born, she no longer remembers the anguish because of the joy of having brought a human being into the world.'

feeling so wretched and sorry for myself, I now knew how fortunate I was.[17]

Towards dawn we had our first visitors – some poor people from the outlying countryside, who tiptoed in while the town was still asleep. They had been told to look for a baby wrapped up and lying in an animals' manger, but since no one else had been to see us it was odd that they knew. They knew the baby was going to save the people, and I told them he was going to be called Jesus, which means Saviour.[18] They might have wondered how we knew, and we might have wondered how they knew, but we all knew our information was reliable. I will never forget the events of that night. It was a time of glory, and a time of peace.[19]

When the baby was eight days old, we took him to be circumcised. It is a good moment, when you know your child now really belongs to the people of God, pledged through the sacrifice of a part of his body to the covenant with God. It is a lifelong commitment, as irreversible as the physical operation, and now I was proud he really was a Jew in every sense of the word. But as I saw him bleed and heard him cry, and as I changed his dressings over the coming days, I thought about him bleeding for the people. Saying yes to God can be a frightening thing. I had said yes to the pregnancy – 'Let your will be done in me', even at the cost of losing my fiancé and incurring public shame (as I then thought), and that had been a frightening step into the unknown. Now my child was pledged, through his circumcision, to accepting the will of God: it was a decision I took on his behalf, and I could not have done otherwise, but it had its frightening side, because from that moment on I never forgot the spilling of his blood.

17 After the birth Mary must really have experienced the truth of Elizabeth's words, 'Blessed are you among women' (Luke 1:42).

18 In Matthew, the angel tells Joseph 'you are to name him Jesus, for he will save his people from their sins' (Matthew 1:21). Luke also works from a tradition in which the name of Jesus is given by God rather than chosen by Mary and Joseph, though here it is Mary who is privileged to receive the message (Luke 1:31).

19 'Glory' and 'peace' are found in the story of the annunciation to the shepherds: 'Glory to God in the highest heaven, and on earth peace among those whom he favours!' (Luke 2:14).

When Jesus was twelve days old we had an unexpected visit from some foreign scholars,[20] who came to visit King Herod first, and then came on to visit my baby. They knew both were kings, you see. They brought Jesus lavish and exotic gifts: an engraved gold box, beautifully smelling incense, and an expensive preservative for anointing dead bodies. I still have them, locked in a wooden trunk Joseph made. There is no sense of luxury like opening that trunk, and breathing in the rich, overpowering smell of the frankincense and myrrh, and seeing the shimmer of the gold,[21] and remembering the words of the foreigners as they gathered awestruck around the crib, that this baby was born to be king of the Jews, and the shepherd of the people.

A few weeks later we took him to the temple in Jerusalem for my purification after the birth,[22] and a man there took Jesus in his arms and told me that a sword would pierce my heart. My whole life has been like that, living with the unexpected, knowing that the good times are for a while only, waiting for the next sacrifice,

20 According to the gospel account, they were not kings but 'wise people' (Matthew 2:1). Neither their number nor their sex is given (the masculine plural only implies that at least one of them was male), though given the cultural setting of the day, in which women were not normally educated, it would be quite likely that they were all men.

21 It could be intriguing to speculate on what happened to the gold, frankincense and myrrh. If they ever existed, they would probably have been carefully preserved by the mother, as today's christening presents most frequently are.

22 Luke's account of the visit to the temple in 2:22–39 appears to combine two religious ceremonies, the redemption of a first-born male (see Exodus 13:1, 11–16), and the purification of the mother after giving birth (which is laid down in Leviticus 12, with the prescribed offering of a pair of turtledoves, which Mary offered). Usually the occasion is referred to as the Presentation, thereby placing emphasis on the male child, but I have chosen rather to recover the dimension of the woman's experience by giving priority to the Purification. (By doing this I do not, of course, wish in any way to imply that childbirth is polluting or that a purification is the most appropriate way for a woman to commemorate a birth before God.)

anticipating bloodshed. That does not mean my life has been unhappy, rather that joy has an edge of fragility to it, and sorrow a depth of peace to it. 'Let your will be done, I will serve you in whatever way you want.' That prayer is my deepest security, deeper than the presence of husband or son.

I did not have long to wait until disaster struck. King Herod, who had been expecting the foreigners to go back and make a report to him, flew into a fury when he realized they had given him the slip. I can hardly bear to speak of what happened next, because I know that hundreds of babies – every boy under two years old in the Bethlehem district – were murdered by his soldiers. It was Jesus they were looking for, and because Joseph and I fled with him, those innocent children died in his place. It has been hard to live with the guilt. If I had given up my son, their lives would have been spared. To save one child, hundreds had to be killed. The burden of those deaths has never left me, and I hardly dared to enjoy watching my own child play when I thought of it. I did not kill them, but I could have saved their lives if I had given up my son – who was the one Herod was looking for.

These, though, are the reflections of later years. I had not the energy at that time to feel guilty about the slaughter left behind us. All I knew then was the sudden message that the soldiers were coming down the road, killing children, and Joseph and I picked up Jesus and ran. We fled for days on end, exhausted, famished, not daring to stop until we were out of the country ruled by Herod. You will understand how desperate we were when I tell you that we fled into Egypt – the historical land of our people's slavery, from which we had escaped with such effort so many years ago.[23] In Egypt now we had nothing, no money, no home, no knowledge of the language, no shared faith. Luckily Joseph had carpentry skills that could get him work, and we survived. We lived. Jesus lived. We felt like the birds of the air, or the flowers of the field, just alive for today, with no idea what would happen tomorrow. But tomorrow came, and we were still alive. There was a freedom in that – to put all our trust in God alone. Again my prayer was important, 'Let your will be done. I will serve you in whatever way

⧈

---

23 Moses led the Jews out of slavery in Egypt, as the book of Exodus records.

you want.' If we live, I told myself, it will be because God feeds us, and God clothes us. And God did.[24]

When Jesus was two we heard that Herod had died. It was one of those reversals of fortune so typical of the way God works. Herod had tried to kill my son, and now my son was alive and Herod dead. It was great news for us in Egypt: as far as we knew we could have been there all our lives, though I kept going by taking it a day at a time and trying not to think how long it might continue. What joy it was to come back: every step of the way was a step towards home, and I relished the travel and the sights and the villages. We went and settled in Nazareth, and there, with our two-year-old son, we made a permanent home at last.

The next 28 years were the happiest of my life. Joseph made furniture, so he was always at home with us. Jesus grew in grace and strength, and every age seemed more glorious than the last. As I looked at him, toddling down the road, or going fishing for tadpoles, or climbing trees, I could see he was my son: he had my nose and my chin, my hair and my stride. And day by day, year by year, I basked in the daily presence of God. The sun seemed always to be touching the stones with gold – and I remembered the gold hidden in the trunk. The wild flowers seemed always to be giving off their fragrance – and I thought of the sweet frankincense and myrrh in the trunk.

One of my great joys was teaching Jesus to read, as my mother had taught me to read at her knee.[25] And I taught him how to

24 'Do not worry about your life, what you will eat or what you will drink, or about your body, what you will wear. . . . Look at the birds of the air. . . . Consider the lilies of the field. . . . Strive first for the reign of God and for God's righteousness, and all these things will be given to you as well' (Matthew 6:25–33). If Jesus had indeed endured a period of refugee existence as a young child, then these words acquire added poignancy. Given his young age during the exile, much of the experience would have been recalled to him through the memories of his mother.

25 There is a tradition in iconography that shows Anna and Mary with a book, as mother teaches daughter to read. Examples can be found in a prayerbook given to Queen Margaret of Scotland by her father Henry VII, in thirteenth-century manuscripts at the Bodleian Library, Oxford, and in a sixteenth-century statue in the Gesù church in Rome.

pray, especially my prayer 'Let your will be done', which had sustained me through my pregnancy, and 'May your reign come', which was special to me because Jesus was the king who would bring in the reign of God. We prayed for our daily food, remembering our days in Egypt when we lived hand to mouth. And in memory of Herod's assassination attempt we prayed to be delivered from evil, as we had been in the past.[26] I was always honest with Jesus, of course, about Joseph not being his father. And, because he knew

More examples are found from the fifteenth century on, as veneration of St Anna increased. This is such a splendid tradition – affirming both learning and teaching as women's work – that I have chosen to make good use of it, irrespective of whether it was culturally likely that women in Jesus' day could read or had reading matter at home. From the tradition that Anna taught Mary to read I develop the idea that Mary likewise taught Jesus to read. From that I go on to suggest that she was the more educated partner in the marriage, and (since it is easy to assume her preferred reading matter was religious) that she had an interest in what today we would call theology, and so stimulated her son's evident passion for the subject.

In the course of a thorough and authoritative survey of the position of Jewish women in Jesus' day, Ben Witherington III reports that there are cases of women being taught the oral law and even being consulted on its fine points. But he also reports the saying that teaching one's daughter Torah [the Law] is teaching her lechery (or extravagance), although he adds that this opinion is believed by Jewish scholars to be a minority one. He concludes, 'Apart from the role of the woman in the home in giving her children some basic religious instruction (and even this was disputed), a woman had no educational functions except in very rare cases' (Women in the Ministry of Jesus, Cambridge University Press, 1984, p. 6). We can perhaps say that it was improbable but not totally inconceivable that Mary had the sort of theological influence upon Jesus that I have chosen to attribute to her.

26 All of these petitions come from the prayer known as the 'Our Father', or the 'Lord's Prayer', which is given in Matthew 6:9–13. By reflecting on the prayer in the light of Jesus' upbringing and from his mother's perspective, we gain fresh insights on what the prayer may have meant to Jesus and how it could have grown out of his childhood experiences.

that, he began from a very early age to pray to God as his father.[27]

We had some scrolls at home and there were others in the synagogue. As Jesus got older we spent hours getting to know the scriptures by heart, and learning about the different interpretations. Joseph was the practical one of the family, and I was the one who introduced Jesus to theology, which became a burning passion in him. He could make a table too, and as he grew up he worked contentedly enough alongside Joseph to support the family.[28] But it did not fulfil him: there was so much left over, so many dreams to live out, so many arguments to work through. He loved an intellectual challenge, and could defeat anyone he took on,[29] and all the time he turned a chair leg his mind would be wrestling with what God was asking of his people in our day.

Only once in those years did something really dreadful happen, when Jesus was twelve.[30] Every year we used to go to Jerusalem at Passover time. It was an annual pilgrimage, and a holiday as

27 As regards the opening words of the prayer, 'Our Father', Joachim Jeremias has observed that 'God is seldom spoken of as "Father" in the Old Testament, in fact only fifteen times', and yet 'no less than 170 times in the gospels, we find the word "Father" for God on the lips of Jesus'. He says that 'whereas there is not a single instance of God being addressed as Abba in the literature of Jewish prayer, Jesus always addressed him in this way (with the exception of the cry from the cross, Mark 15:34 par.). So we have here a quite unmistakeable characteristic of the *ipsissima vox Jesu* [the authentic voice of Jesus]' (*The Prayers of Jesus*, Studies in Biblical Theology, second series, 6, SCM, 1967, pp. 12, 29, 57).

28 Jesus is himself described as a carpenter in Mark 6:3.

29 We see Jesus winning arguments with gusto in, for example, Luke 20:1–8 (on the source of his authority), in Luke 20:20–26 (on paying tribute to Caesar) and Luke 20:27–40 (on marriage in heaven). (All have parallels in Matthew and Mark.) We are told, 'they were not able in the presence of the people to trap him by what he said; and being amazed by his answer they fell silent' (Luke 20:26), and 'they no longer dared to ask him another question' (Luke 20:40).

30 This story comes from Luke 2:41–51.

well, and we would take all the family[31] and travel in a big group
of friends and neighbours and relatives. The temple services gave
a great spiritual lift, and helped me get through the ordinariness
– the blessed but uneventful ordinariness – of the rest of the year.
We always looked forward to our pilgrimage to Jerusalem, and the
journey became very familiar to us – every resting place, every
village. It would take us several days each way. We would travel
in a loose conglomeration of groups, and often the children would
run ahead of us, in the way children do.

31 Whether Jesus had sisters and brothers is not an easy question.
Matthew and Mark tell us unambiguously that he did, and we are given
the names of the brothers, though not (typically) the names of the
sisters. 'Is not this the carpenter, the son of Mary and brother of James
and Joses and Judas and Simon, and are not his sisters here with us?'
(Mark 6:3). 'Is not this the carpenter's son? Is not his mother called
Mary? And are not his brothers James and Joseph and Simon and Judas?
And are not all his sisters with us?' (Matthew 13:55–56). Jesus' sisters
and brothers (or just brothers, the Greek could mean either) are also
mentioned as accompanying Mary, his mother, when she tried to visit
Jesus in the course of his ministry (Matthew 12:46–50, Mark 3:31–35,
Luke 8:19–21). John, too, says he had sisters and brothers (or just
brothers): 'He went down to Capernaum with his mother, his [sisters
and] brothers, and his disciples; and they remained there a few days'
(John 2:12).

John tells us that they were not believers: 'So his [sisters and]
brothers said to him, "Leave here and go to Judaea so that your
disciples also may see the works you are doing; for no one who wants
to be widely known acts in secret. If you do these things, show
yourself to the world." (For not even his [sisters and] brothers believed
in him.) Jesus said to them, "My time has not yet come. . . . Go to the
festival yourselves. . . ." But after his [sisters and] brothers had gone
to the festival, then he also went, not publicly but as it were in secret'
(John 7:3–10). Mark also suggests that Jesus' siblings were not entirely
supportive, in that his family tried to restrain him in some of the supposed excesses of his ministry (Mark 3:21, 31). Both Tertullian and
St John Chrysostom took the view that Mary, too, was an unbeliever
for a while.

But the author of Acts (who also wrote Luke) presents the
family as believers, at least after the resurrection, when they prayed
in the upper room: 'All these were constantly devoting themselves
to prayer, together with certain women, including Mary the mother

of Jesus, as well as his [sisters and] brothers' (Acts 1:14). So too does Paul: 'Do we not have the right to be accompanied by a sister as wife [Greek: a sister a wife], as do the other apostles and the brothers of the Lord and Cephas?' (1 Corinthians 9:5). And he confirms that one of the brothers' names was James: 'I did go up to Jerusalem to visit Cephas and stayed with him fifteen days; but I did not see any other apostle except James the Lord's brother' (Galatians 1:19).

What then is the problem? There are difficulties that arise both from within scripture and from without. From within scripture there is the difficulty that John 19:27, if taken literally, could suggest that by the time of the crucifixion Mary is living alone. Why else does Jesus wish to bequeath her a proxy son in his place, so that the beloved disciple, on Jesus' authority, takes her to live with him (John 19:26–27)? (But see note 50 on p. 49.) Had all the sisters and brothers by this date become wandering apostles, leaving Mary alone? If there were other children, was it not surprising that someone from outside the family should be delegated to care for her? (But see note 51 on p. 49 for the theological interpretation of this saying, which may overcome the problem, though Ben Witherington takes the view that the incident is both theological and historical: *Women in the Ministry of Jesus*, pp. 93–4.)

There is also the difficulty from within scripture that people called James and Joses (or Joseph) and Judas (or Jude), who are related to each other and who are part of the early Christian community, are mentioned quite frequently, but they are not children of Mary and Joseph. This gives rise to the suggestion that the so-called sisters and brothers of Jesus are in fact close relatives, rather than full siblings. In a world where the extended family was the norm, it is possible that cousins who grew up with Jesus might be described loosely as his sisters and brothers, meaning simply 'others from his family'. This view, that the 'sisters and brothers' are cousins, was first put forward by Jerome in AD 382.

Another theory, which was developed by Epiphanius in AD 376–377, suggested that they were children of Joseph by a previous marriage, and therefore older half-sisters and half-brothers. There is support for this in some non-scriptural documents, *The Gospel of the Hebrews*, *The Gospel of Peter*, and *The Proto-Evangelium of James*.

The texts in question, with their complicated family networks, are as follows. (Of course we do not know how many different people of the same name are referred to.) Judas had a brother called James (Jude 1:1). Judas (the apostle but not Iscariot) had a father called James (Luke 6:16, Acts 1:13). James had a father called Alphaeus, and his name is mentioned alongside that of Simon and Judas (Mark 3:18, Luke 6:15, Acts 1:13). James had a brother called Joses, and a mother called Mary who is not the mother of Jesus (Matthew 27:56, Mark 15:40). It

One year, when Jesus was twelve, we had been journeying back a day and a half, thinking Jesus was in one or other of the groups ahead of us, before we discovered for sure that he was not with the party at all. It was difficult to be certain, you see: you walked faster to catch up with the group ahead, only to find he was not there, and

may well be this same Mary (because she had the same name and was in the same place at the same time, i.e. under the cross) who was the wife of Clopas (John 19:25).

The problem from outside of scripture is that there is a long and tenacious tradition that Mary, the mother of Jesus, remained a virgin throughout her life. Exploring this, we can ask what this tradition meant and what it stood for. The traditional answer is that Mary's perpetual virginity was a sign of her total purity and sinlessness and her complete commitment to God. Nowadays, however, perpetual virginity for a married woman is not seen as a sign of any of those things; it is more likely to be seen as an indication that she needs some psycho-sexual counselling. We need to ask, therefore, whether the tradition of Mary's perpetual virginity has today quite the same force, necessity and significance that it once had for Christians.

Nonetheless, oral traditions need to be treated with great respect, and we should not accept the assumption that a tradition which is unwritten is worthless. I have, for example, followed the oral tradition that Jesus met Mary as he was carrying his cross: see note 43 on p. 46.

A further consideration worth noting is the beginning of a new, positive, feminist value being given to the concept of virginity, which could give a new perspective to devotion to the Blessed Virgin Mary. Jane Schaberg, for example, describes how a virgin can be seen as 'a woman never subdued', a woman who is 'undefeated, integral, and creative, one who is not identified or destroyed by her relationship with men' (The Illegitimacy of Jesus, p. 198). Virginity, perhaps, needs to be understood more widely as a moral and spiritual category, rather than as a mere biological fact. In this broader interpretation, perhaps, we could find a sense in which the credal belief that Jesus was 'born of the virgin Mary' could retain a moral truth even if Mary was raped, as Schaberg suggests she may have been (see note 2 on p. 22 above). Clearly a raped woman is morally equivalent to a virgin, since there can be no sin in being the victim of violence. It would be deeply unchristian to see a rape victim as defiled.

In avoiding explicit mention of other children, I have tried to leave this chapter open to either possibility – that Mary had other children or that she did not.

then you had to run ahead to catch up with the even more energetic walkers ahead of them. It took a long time to get right to the front, since Joseph and I were not the most athletic, and we had to overtake those who were far more fit than we were. And then we had to sit still and wait while all the other groups passed us again, before we could be certain Jesus was nowhere in the caravan.

I could not believe I had lost him, after I had kept him safe through all our time as refugees. We had to turn round and go back to Jerusalem, and we looked in all the streets, and we looked in the place we had stayed in, and he was not there. I was getting more and more anxious, and kept on worrying that I had lost him for good – he might have been kidnapped or murdered or something and how would we ever know? I said to Joseph we must go to the temple and place our petition before God, and when we got there, there was Jesus, surrounded by scribes, talking theology with them.

'Why, why, why have you done this to us?', I asked, 'Don't you know how worried we have been?' And Jesus, all calm and collected, as though spending days in the temple was the most normal thing in the world, said 'Didn't you know I would be in my father's house?'[32] By his 'father', of course, he meant God. And so I learnt that the temple was a second home to him. I remembered that twenty years later, when he spent long days in the temple, talking theology again, but this time teaching people rather than wrestling out questions with the theologians.[33] I remembered it also, when he made a whip of cords and started driving people out of the temple because he thought they were misusing the sacred space.[34]

32   The Greek is capable of two translations: 'in my father's house' or 'about my father's business'.

33   Luke 19:47 tells us, 'Every day he was teaching in the temple' (see also Luke 21:37). Matthew and Mark report Jesus saying that he taught in the temple day after day (Matthew 26:55, Mark 14:49). John also speaks of him repeatedly teaching in the temple: 'Early in the morning he came again to the temple. All the people came to him and he sat down and began to teach them' (John 8:2).

34   This disturbing story is one of the best attested incidents from Jesus' life, recorded in all four gospels: Matthew 21:12–13; Mark 11:15–19; Luke 19:45–47; John 2:13–17.

He felt he had a right to do that, because it was his home and they were abusing his hospitality.

I am slipping now into the next stage of my life, the stage when Jesus left. I knew the time had to come, because he could not save the people or be the king just living at home with me all the time. But when he went I felt my heart would break. Joseph by now had died,[35] which meant I felt all the more bereft when Jesus left me too. We were so happy together, though I knew much of him was unfulfilled, and he was becoming restless. When he went, he really went, it seemed he had to cut me right out of his life, almost that he had to hate me.[36] I think he felt home was a temptation, and that he had to root out the comfort and security of it to commit himself to living on the road.[37]

The first thing I knew about him going was when he told me he was going to be baptized by John. Now I had known John as a newborn baby – he was Elizabeth's child, and I had been there when he was born. After that the years ran past and I did not see him until suddenly I realized that he had grown up and become famous as a Baptizer and Prophet. Jesus did not know his cousin, but he identified with his message of repentance and he wanted to receive his baptism. He said goodbye to me, and went, and already I suspected that he would not come back.

∞

35 Tradition has sometimes assumed that Joseph was considerably older than Mary – probably as a way of explaining why he did not mind renouncing an active sex life. But since women tend to live longer than men we do not need to rely on such a theory to hypothesize that he had died by the time of Jesus' ministry, during which period we hear news of Mary but not of Joseph. The only passage that might imply Joseph was still alive is John 6:42, 'Is not this Jesus, the son of Joseph, whose father and mother we know?', but against that we must set the marriage at Cana in John 2, when 'the mother of Jesus was there' but there is no mention of Joseph.

36 Jesus talks of the need to 'hate' your own family in order to be free for the gospel: 'Whoever comes to me and does not hate father and mother, wife and children, brothers and sisters, yes, and even life itself, cannot be my disciple' (Luke 14:26).

37 Jesus' homeless condition is referred to in the saying: 'Foxes have holes, and birds of the air have nests; but the Son of Man has nowhere to lay his head' (Matthew 8:20; Luke 9:58). ·

After he went I heard nothing for a couple of months. It seemed Jesus actually disappeared after he was baptized by Elizabeth's son John, and no one knew where he was. But eventually I heard he was back in the neighbouring city of Capernaum with some of his new friends that he had picked up in the south of the country and from the circle of John. There was a wedding coming up in the next town of Cana, so I sent word to Jesus that he was invited along with me, and for the sake of his dear friends who were marrying he turned up, along with a few friends. That was when he began to speak to me in a distant way. I asked him to help them out, because they had run out of wine and he said to me bluntly, 'So what, woman?' All the same, he did help them out.

A couple of weeks later he came to synagogue back in Nazareth, and went forward to read and then comment on the scripture. His words were captivating. I looked round, at all our relatives and friends and neighbours. Their eyes were fixed on him, and every word he said sunk in. But suddenly he began to push them too far, as he spoke about the gentiles being favoured over the Jews, and they got angry. They were saying, 'This is only Jesus, the son of the carpenter, who grew up with us. Who on earth does he think he is, going on at us as though he were telling us off?' There was a note of such authority, you see, when he spoke, as though he knew everything, and they resented it, and some even began to say it was blasphemous, and before I knew what was happening they were hauling him out of the synagogue and saying he should be thrown off the cliff. I was there, in the congregation, watching this, embarrassed and terrified. Once again I began to think he would die, before his time had come. I remembered the blood of his circumcision and knew I had to give him up willingly, but I still was afraid that his work was barely started, let alone finished. Thank God he gave them the slip. But he never came back to Nazareth again.

The next years were difficult for me. Not only did I have to live alone, but I felt an enemy in my own town, since the inhabitants had tried to murder my son. I would hear of his doings, and he became more and more famous, and more and more controversial. I rejoiced in the will of God, because he was doing great things for God, and that was why he had been brought into the world, that was why I had nurtured him, and brought him up, and taught him, and prepared him – all for this moment, and what he was doing was so important. But it hurt that he never came home again. It was as though he wanted to shake the dust of Nazareth off his feet.

For a while he worked in Galilee, not in Nazareth itself, but in the neighbouring towns, like Capernaum and Bethsaida, and his ministry went very well. I went out to join him there from time to time. It was easy to find him, he was notorious and there were always huge crowds. But it was not always a satisfactory meeting, and I remember one occasion as particularly painful, when I had gone to look for him with some other relations. We found someone on the edge of the crowd and asked her to send word in to Jesus that his mother and family were here. We could not see him for the crowd, but could hear his voice teaching, and then there was a mumble as the message was passed to him. Then we heard his voice boom out, 'Who are my mother and my family? All who hear the word of God are my mother and family.' For the first time I felt I was a burden to him.

All the same, he did come and find me later on, when he had sent the crowds away, and he talked to me about the wider family, and about the need to leave mother and family behind. He said it was not just something he had to do, in following the call of God, but something I had to do as well, in being prepared to let him go. He said our brothers and sisters, parents and children had to go beyond blood kinship; everyone who was a child of God was our sister or brother, our mother or child, and in this way the family we lost for the sake of the kingdom was replaced by a much bigger family if only we could open our hearts to them. I could not help feeling that must be a lot easier for someone who does not have Jesus as their son. How could anyone else take his place?

I went back to Nazareth, because I did not want to be an encumbrance, and I did not want him to feel I could not accept the call of God. It is funny, isn't it? Some people were called to leave all and follow him, and that seemed to me so easy, compared to the other call, to leave Jesus and go back home. Of course there is always a lot of work to do for God. There are always a lot of people needing help of one kind or another, and I had a lot to give, because of my knowledge of the scriptures and because I had the time. But it is hard when there is a gap in your life, and the one person you want to be with, at every moment, is absent.

And it was also hard for me because of the clash Jesus had had with the people of Nazareth. The town was divided about him, and that made it hard for me. Instead of being just an ordinary person who could offer help where needed, I was always the mother of Jesus. With some people, that made new opportunities, because they wanted to talk to me about him and his teaching. But for others, it marked me off as suspect. And for everyone, it turned me into a sort of quasi-celebrity, so there was a kind of distance between me and others. If it had not been for God's plan and Jesus' vocation, it would have been nice to have followed the usual course of life, and seen Jesus marry and have children.[38] It was not just that I would have liked to have been a mother-in-law and grandmother, but that Jesus loved children so much. He had such energy and patience with them, and would go on playing and telling them stories after everyone else was tired. He would have been a wonderful father. He would have been a wonderful husband too: he treated women as equals.

Gradually, over the three years of his work, he spent more time in the south, and less in Galilee, and that is when I missed him most. It was an anxious time, for he was a far more controversial figure down there, and it was not long before the rumours came of a plot on his life.

That Passover I went to Jerusalem, as I always did, and at least I was able to see Jesus in his last days, even if not alone. By this time his movements had to be very secret, and it was only in the big public situations that I could be sure of seeing him, and then there was no opportunity for a private word. But at least I was there. Many people that year were talking about how he had raised Lazarus from the dead at Bethany: that household had become almost an adopted family for him, I felt, where he had made deep

38 The only argument that can be adduced in favour of Jesus being married is that most people were. Against him having a wife are the following considerations. Jesus was clearly unconventional and challenged the customary cultural assumptions. There is no reference to any wife in the New Testament, although the gospels try to report very fully on his life. When they refer to other members of his family, as they do on several occasions, no wife is mentioned. Most importantly, Jesus had a strong sense of mission that drove him to disregard the normal urge to settle down in family life: his priorities lay elsewhere. And so, though we cannot prove that he was unmarried, there are no grounds for suggesting that he was and every reason to believe that he was not.

Ben Witherington stresses the importance of Jesus' view that the single state was a legitimate calling: 'it was this teaching which made it possible for women also to assume roles other than those of wife and mother in Jesus' community' (*Women in the Ministry of Jesus*, p. 125).

personal ties and could thoroughly relax. The story I heard of Lazarus being raised from the dead made me think that Jesus had become a mother, bringing new life out of the darkness of the tomb, as once I had brought new life out of the darkness of my womb. Lazarus had become a son to Jesus, the first that he had called out of darkness into light, as he was to call many others, and in a more permanent way, as he called them not just to a few more years on earth but to eternal life.

However, it was not just admirers who were talking about the raising of Lazarus. This was the last straw as far as his enemies were concerned, for a man who had a reputation for bringing the dead to life was a most powerful threat both to the Romans – who feared his sense of invulnerability would impel him to lead the people to revolution – and to the temple authorities – who totally refused to consider the possibility that he might be the Messiah. In the week leading up to the Passover I had a strong sense that we had reached the end, and it was a race against time to see if Jesus would ever reach the Passover at the end of the week.

Accounts of Jesus' activity grew wilder and wilder. It was said a woman had spent a year's income[39] on a single jar of ointment that she had poured over Jesus' body as he sat at a meal, and he had given explicit approval to this. It was also in this week that he rampaged in the temple, driving people out with a whip, and that was an incident I witnessed myself, to my horror and fear and incomprehension. I had a better clue to understanding it than anyone, because I knew he had always seen the temple as his father's house, but it was still a shocking event.

I heard his last speeches in the temple – delivered with a passion and desperation never reached before, full of insulting attacks on the chief priests and terrifying stories of what would happen in the end times. In that last week, when he prepared for his arrest, even his most unquestioning admirers – and who could be more so than a mother? – found themselves frightened. We

39 The ointment was worth 300 denarii, according to Mark 14:5 and John 12:5, and a denarius was the daily wage of a working man. I have made Mary of Nazareth unaware of the identity of the woman who anointed Jesus, just as Matthew and Mark were unaware, although elsewhere in this book I have followed John in identifying her as Mary of Bethany. See the chapter on Mary of Bethany.

wondered if he had not, after all, gone too far. And yet what would be appalling behaviour by anyone else had a compelling authority when it was done by Jesus.

The end came. I was in the crowd outside Pilate's palace, hearing the blood cries bellowing through the mass of people. I saw the mindless way in which those who wanted a good shout would pick up any refrain and use it as an exercise for their lungs. You know what they shouted.[40] I do not wish to repeat it.

I walked with my son up the hill to his execution. If I had a sword of steel piercing my heart[41] it could not have been more painful to make the journey. At one point I begged the soldiers to let me go to him, just after he had fallen down under the weight of his cross. They were pushing me roughly away but I saw the centurion[42] and appealed to him: 'I'm his mother.' He escorted me himself, and turned his back discreetly while I went to Jesus.[43] I knelt on the road beside him and held his hand, and we looked at each other in silence. Then he spoke. 'It has to be', he said. I said to him, 'I know.' Then I said, 'It has to be because I named you Jesus, the one who saves.'[44] He kept his eyes on me and said the words of the prayer I taught him, 'Let your will be done in me'. And I kept my eyes on him and echoed back at him the next line, 'I will serve you in whatever way you wish'. And we knelt there, on the hard road under the blazing sun, watched by hundreds of jeering onlookers, looking at each other stupidly, with tears and sweat coursing down our faces – and blood too in his case – and that I think was our closest moment. All those happy years in Nazareth of growing up in the service of God had just been theory

---

40 'Away with him! Away with him! Crucify him!' (John 19:15).

41 Simeon said to Mary when she presented her baby son in the temple, 'A sword will pierce your own soul too' (Luke 2:35).

42 Later the centurion was to acknowledge Jesus as son of God, when he saw the way he died (Matthew 27:54; Mark 15:39).

43 Though it does not appear as an incident in the gospels, the ancient tradition of the Stations of the Cross records a moment on the way to Calvary when Jesus meets his mother.

44 'Jesus' means the one who saves: see note 18 on p. 31 above.

and preparation for this. From that moment the journey was a little easier for me, and I was able to reach the top of the hill, but for him, maybe, it was more difficult, because he had the added burden of knowing that I saw it all. But at least we both knew, after all the misunderstandings, that when it came to the end we both understood.

At the top of the hill they made him take his clothes off. I was the one who knew him from a child in his nakedness, and our privacy was violated on that hill. The rest became a blanket of pain that I will not speak about.[45] I had nightmares for a long time after. In my dreams I see a dark curtain and wonder what is behind it. And then I see lumps dripping down it, and I wonder what they are, until I see they are reddish, and realize they are blood. And then the curtain rips violently open[46] and there is a light that blinds my eyes and a screaming that will not stop. And I am left in terror even after I have woken, because I know I had not seen anything yet of what there was to see.

Or I have another dream, in which we are in Nazareth, and Jesus is sawing a plank, and he asks me to hold it while he saws. And as I hold it he saws through my hand on the wood, without noticing, and I try to tell him but I cannot make my voice come out. And I struggle to scream out, until I wake up with a cry.

Or I have a third dream, an identification parade, in which I am made to walk right in front of a line of crosses, and all I can see are the feet, dangling at my eye level, each one nailed onto the wood, and each one bleeding and twitching. And they say to me before each foot, 'Is this one your son? Is this one your son?'

45 In iconography, Mary is often shown at the foot of the cross in a swoon of pain.

46 At Jesus' death, 'the curtain of the temple was torn in two' (Luke 23:45). The author of the epistle to the Hebrews interprets this theologically, as showing that we obtain access to God through the death of Jesus: 'we have confidence to enter the sanctuary by the blood of Jesus, by the new and living way that he opened for us through the curtain (that is, through his flesh)' (Hebrews 10:19–20).

But I do have one clear memory from the hill, that I will share with you. All the time there were strong and gentle hands holding me, and usually I did not even know whose hands they were, except that they bore my weight at a time when I had not the strength to stand.[47] There were a lot of friends there, Salome, and Mary of Magdala, and the other Mary, and my sister.[48] But all those new men friends of Jesus – all those twelve brave men whom he chose to carry on his work – they all ran away, except one. And the one who stayed was Jesus' special friend, whom he loved. While we stood there, Jesus spoke to me one last time, breathing out his words in pain, but desperate to get through one last message. He

47 In pictures of the crucifixion, the swooning Mary is held up by her friends.

Elisabeth Moltmann-Wendel is dubious about the picture of Jesus' mother as faithful disciple who stood by him at the foot of the cross. She contrasts her unfavourably with Mary of Magdala, about whom she believes there is a stronger biblical tradition of fidelity. She writes (with a fair degree of imaginative reconstruction, which may or may not be plausible):

'According to the biblical narratives, Mary Magdalene was the woman who stood closest to Jesus. Mary, the mother of Jesus, in no way played this role, which was ascribed to her later. She regarded her son as a frivolous character (Mark 3:21) whom she would really have liked to have taken in hand. The early Church always found it a source of great grief that Mary thought so little of the Jesus movement. The fact was hushed up, played down, and finally the evangelist John placed her under the cross. Perhaps this is a hint at her later understanding of the unusual course taken by her son. Luke, too, is aware of the belated recognition of Jesus by his family, and their role in the primitive community (Acts 1:14). However, the woman who stood by Jesus throughout his life, sensitive and understanding, was Mary Magdalene' (The Women Around Jesus, p. 65).

See also note 31 on p. 37 above on Jesus' family.

48 See note 2 on p. 116 in the chapter on Mary of Magdala, and note 31 above, for the suggested identification of 'the other Mary' with Mary the mother of James and Joses, and with Mary the wife of Clopas. I have preferred the term 'the other Mary' because it does not name her after a male figure. The gospel references for these women at the cross are Matthew 27:56, Mark 15:40, Luke 23:49 and John 19:25. See also Luke 24:10.

said 'Woman, look at your son.'[49] And he said to the friend he loved: 'Look at your mother.' I looked at his friend whose hands were holding me at that moment, and he looked at me, and I remembered what Jesus had always told me about finding new sisters and brothers, mothers and children, among those who were God's children. And instead of feeling hurt and insulted that my own son was leaving me and giving me someone else as substitute, I was so weak and needy in that moment that I realized how desperately each one of us needs all the family we can have in this cruel life. From that day he took me to himself, made me at home where he lived,[50] and treated me with the respect he would show to his own mother. I love him, as Jesus' own brother, and because of Jesus there is a strong sense of a common family bond between us while he is away.[51]

49 John Peter Lange, in his 1872 commentary, thinks that the word 'woman' is used because it 'denotes particularly the character of woman in her helplessness and need of comfort'. It is chance remarks like these, made in all innocence, that open a window onto the depth of sexist prejudice that has distorted our reading of the gospels for centuries.

50 The Greek is less specific and concrete than the customary English translation of 'took her into his own home' (John 19:27). More literally it says he 'took her to his own', and perhaps does not necessarily entail Mary moving into his house. The same phrase is used in John 1:11: 'He came to what was his own, and his own people did not accept him.'

51 This is the interpretation favoured by the Canadian theologian Mary T. Malone: 'The whole Crucifixion scene in John is constructed for precise theological reasons; it is hardly likely that this Marian scene has any other intent. What then is the reason? Here at the foot of the Cross are two persons with no personal names, a woman and a man. The woman is called the "mother of Jesus", "woman", and "mother". The man is called "beloved disciple" and "son". Here, again, is the mystery of relationship. These persons are placed here to play symbolic roles, roles that have to do with the "hour" of Jesus, roles, therefore, that point forward to the new community and do not look back on the past. Before Jesus' work is completed, the new community must be brought into being. Here is the Church, the new creation symbolically represented at the foot of the Cross. Here is a

While Jesus was on the cross I was willing him to die, so he would be out of his agony, and it seemed to take forever. And yet after he breathed his last breath I wanted him still to be alive. Where there is some life there is hope, but when he died I felt more barren and empty than I could have believed possible. My friends sat me on the ground and after they had taken down the body they laid it in my lap. I held it and tried to stroke his skin into life and I wound my fingers in his matted hair. I wanted to get his blood on me and make myself dirty and polluted with it, so that my appearance would match the wretchedness of my feelings. I thought, 'My baby is dead.' I offered to God this poor dead baby of mine, who was also God's baby. 'Take my son', I said, then 'Take your son.' And I told God that he was so trampled in the dust that there was no lower place in the universe he could have sunk to than this.[52] And I prayed that salvation would come out of this appalling evil. I prayed that God would overturn the situation, bring down those who had murdered Jesus, and raise my son from the dust of death and dishonour.

On the third day . . . you know the rest. God showed mighty strength, and scattered the proud who had imagined they had sorted out the situation and put an end to Jesus. God brought down the powerful – the high priest and the Roman governors – and raised up Jesus from the dust of death. God filled the grieving followers of Jesus with joy and satisfied their hunger for justice in a way that exceeded all expectations. Everything Jesus' enemies thought they had achieved in putting him to death was overthrown,

small representative community of believing disciples, with new bonds of relationship forged from the life, death, and resurrection of Jesus. It is not surprising that in the following vignette we hear Jesus say that all is now completed. His work has been accomplished. The "mother" and the "son" are model foundation stones of the Church. . . . At Calvary, we see a new community, a new People of God and a new family. It is no accident that the early Christians called each other by these names – mother, sister, brother, father' (Who Is My Mother?, p. 115).

52 The apostles' creed contains the phrase 'he descended into hell', to which various interpretations can be given. One of them is that Jesus went through the worst and most degrading experiences that any human being can ever have.

and their apparent victory was revealed as an empty sham. Those who had served God were helped and we were shown yet again that we had a God of mercy. The promise made to Abraham was fulfilled, when God said, 'I will establish my covenant between me and you, and your offspring after you throughout their generations.' And the promise made to Sarah came to pass, when God said, 'I will bless her, and she shall give rise to nations; kings of peoples shall come from her.' If ever my soul sang for joy it was then.[53]

When I saw Jesus after he rose it felt so normal, so natural, it was as though what was odd was that no one had believed him before. And though the nightmares continued for a while – because of the horror of what I had seen with my own eyes – when I woke I was overcome by the joy of how things had worked out. I do not think it is possible to be more exhausted, first from grief and then from excitement, than I was in those days. It was really only after Pentecost that I got my energy back.

From Pentecost until now life has never stopped. I stand at the beginning of a new age, and the followers of Jesus grow in number day by day. When I saw the work of Jesus was being carried on, I lost any resentment about the way the twelve had deserted him before. I saw they were changed – there was even a change in the constitution of the group[54] – and that they would not fail him again.

And I have been as involved as any of them, for though there are plenty of them to share the story of Jesus' last three years, there is only one of me to tell the story of the 30 years before. I cannot be everywhere, talking to everyone at once, but I do my best, because it is important that Jesus' life is seen as a whole. Otherwise there is a danger of seeing him as a sort of apparition who just materialized at the right moment. But he was a baby, he was a

53 Throughout this paragraph, Mary applies the words of the Magnificat, 'My soul magnifies the Lord' (Luke 1:47–55), to the resurrection experience. The promises to Abraham and Sarah come from Genesis 17:7 and 17:16.

54 Mary alludes indirectly to the painful fact that one of the twelve, Judas Iscariot, who betrayed Jesus, had committed suicide and been replaced by Matthias (Matthew 27:3–5, Acts 1:15–26).

child, he was an adolescent and he was a young adult, and I keep trying to get that message across, even though many of the men seem to undervalue his earlier life and treat it like a domestic detail that is women's stuff. They do not see the importance of the process. They do not realize the beauty of growth and development and change. Jesus was no ready-made prophet. He is seen in terms that are too utilitarian when it is only his last years of ministry that are counted.

People are always fascinated to hear my story, but often they treat it rather like a preliminary to the real stuff, or an optional extra.[55] Of course I have a different way of talking from that of the men. They tend to rattle out a list of Jesus' sayings and teachings, as though the essence of Jesus could be captured by a shorthand reporter. I speak more personally about my experiences.

But they are not just memories: the point is to remember and reflect and draw out the significance of what I saw and heard. My memories of Jesus have been treasured in my heart,[56] cherished and meditated on for years. That is true theology – to experience, to reflect, to live and value the reality, and then out of the richness of one's heart to bring up an eternal truth, drawn out of the human

55 Of the four gospels, only Luke's includes material about the early life of Jesus. The other three gospels begin the account when Jesus is already about 30 years of age. Luke's early chapters may well owe any historical foundation (such as there is) to traditions originating from Jesus' mother, whether directly or indirectly. It is Mary of Nazareth, after all, who is said to have treasured and pondered the events in her heart (see next footnote).

The entire face of Christian tradition has been transformed by Luke's inclusion of this childhood material, for the doctrine of the incarnation proclaims that God is united to the human race not by adopting a virtuous adult male as his Son, but rather by taking on the flesh of a helpless baby in the womb. There are reasons, therefore, to see Mary of Nazareth as one of the most influential theological sources in the history of the Church.

56 When the shepherds visited Jesus on the night of his birth, 'Mary treasured all these words and pondered them in her heart' (Luke 2:19). When Jesus was found in the temple, 'his mother treasured all these things in her heart' (Luke 2:51).

story.[57] And after all, that is the way Jesus taught – through telling stories[58] and reflecting on them.

It always gives me joy to meet the new Christians and see their faces light up when I share my memories and reflections with them. But I am old now and I do look forward to seeing my husband again, and my son again (or 'my eldest son', I should say, as I now live with the new son Jesus gave me – a token of the truth that everyone in the world is part of one family, the family of God).[59]

But though I am always busy, going where my health permits to tell my memories, and welcoming those who come to our house to hear my story, I have the peace of mind of knowing that my life's work is done. It was finished that day on Calvary, when I held my dead son in my arms and offered him to God for the salvation of the world.[60]

57 Mary anticipates the insights of liberation theologians, with the 'pastoral cycle' method, i.e. experience/analysis/theological reflection/action leading to new experience.

58 i.e. the parables.

59 See note 31 on p. 37 above on the question of Jesus' sisters and brothers.
    This is perhaps an appropriate moment to mention the doctrine of the Assumption, which was defined by Pope Pius XII in 1950, and which declares that at her death Mary was assumed body and soul into heaven, thus anticipating the resurrection of the body which awaits all believers in due course. The origins of this belief are very ancient, and can be traced back at least to the fifth century.

60 Jesus' last words on the cross were 'It is finished' (or 'It is accomplished'), according to John 19:30, meaning at one and the same time that his life was over and that the salvation of the world was achieved. The sacrifice of Calvary was once and for all, but Christians have to re-unite themselves constantly with Jesus in offering their lives, with his, to God. In Catholic theology, they do this as a priestly people, through offering the sacrifice of the mass. Mary of Nazareth, as Jesus' mother, present at Calvary itself, was in a unique position to take a lead in offering her son's life to God. That act of offering is the essence of priestly action.

THE STORY OF
PHOTINA

OF SAMARIA
WHO MET A STRANGER AT A WELL

I come from Sychar,[1] in Samaria, and am known as Photina,[2] which means 'woman of light'. I suppose it is a name that suits me, for I have always had an ability to attract a following. From my teens I knew I was attractive, with a slim figure, a pretty face and good teeth. I taught myself to dress well on a modest budget – to match colours, and add different accessories and jewellery so that I had a constant round of new outfits. Why not look good if you can? I am a woman and proud of it, and could never see the point of dressing drably under the banner of modesty. Sexual attractiveness is largely a matter of self-awareness after all, and once you have that you have to be perverse to lose it.

Looking good made me feel good, and so I would laugh and chatter and entertain. Most women are content to act the way they are expected to. They do not speak unless spoken to, they do not go out unless escorted by a man, they do not dare have opinions on how they want to spend their life. I was never prepared to play that game. As a teenager I used to boast to myself that I could go into any group of men and emerge with the one I wanted. I said it to myself as a joke, and it was not always true, but I did not fall far short.

And so I always had a lot of men friends, because I was so outgoing, but some among the girls were jealous. They expressed their envy by saying I was forward.[3] But in this world where

❧

1 Sychar is otherwise known as Sichem, or Shechem – its name in the Old Testament. See also note 12 on p. 62.

2 'Photina' is the Latinization of the Greek form, 'Photeine', which is an adjective meaning 'radiant' or 'shining', from the noun *phōs* (light). Ancient legend, recorded in the Roman Martyrology, ascribes this name to the woman at the well.

    The highly untrustworthy legend goes on to recount that she preached the gospel in various places, went to Carthage, was imprisoned for three years for her faith, and died a martyr. Martyred along with her were her two sons – Joseph and Victor, three sisters – Photis, Parasceve and Cyriaca, and three others – Sebastian, Anatolius and Photius. A further legend from Spain says that Photina converted and baptized Nero's daughter, Domnina, along with a hundred of her servants.

The legend has always been more widespread in the East, and Photeine is still a name that is common among Greek Orthodox women. The saint is commemorated in their calendar, and their important feast of the Fifth Sunday of Easter is centred on this gospel story. The Russian Orthodox translate Photeine as Svetlana. Referring to the meaning of the name, a modern Orthodox writer, Eva Catafygiotu Topping, says: 'The nameless woman of the Gospel becomes transfigured into light, listed in Orthodox liturgical books as the "Glorious Saint and Great Martyr Photeine, the Samaritan woman" ' (*Holy Mothers of Orthodoxy: Women and the Church*, Light and Life Publishing Company, Minneapolis, Minnesota, 1987). See also Topping's subsequent book, *Saints and Sisterhood: the Lives of Forty-Eight Holy Women: A Menologion or Month-by-Month Listing and Study of Women Saints on the Orthodox Calendar* (Light and Life, 1990). And see note 31 on p. 75 below.

Apart from the use of the name Photina, I have not followed the legend in this chapter, because of its doubtful historicity and because I feel it would take me too far from the spirit and style of the gospel story. Though it would be good to gain an African dimension by taking Photina to Carthage, and desirable to boost yet further her reputation as a great preacher and witness, I should then logically have to follow ancient legend in taking Martha and Mary of Bethany on a raft to France, and Mary of Magdala to Provence in the company of her spiritual director Maximinus.

The fact that the name is Greek in style is not necessarily inappropriate, given the Samaritans' capacity to take on Greek names in, for example, the naming of their temple after Zeus Hellenios, see note 16 on p. 66.

3   The assumption has always been that a woman who had had five husbands, and was now living with a man not her husband (John 4:18), must have been more than averagely sexually active, and it is not easy to construct an alternative theory, though Gail R. O'Day rather unconvincingly attempts to do so: 'There are many possible reasons for the woman's marital history, and one should be leery of the dominant explanation of moral laxity. Perhaps the woman, like Tamar in Genesis 38, is trapped in the custom of levirate marriage and the last male in the family line has refused to marry her' (*Women's Bible Commentary*, p. 296).

In this book I have tried to represent a broad sweep of women, of different ages, personalities and lifestyles. Highly sexed women are as much a part of the female race as are high-minded women,

women are undervalued and shut up indoors I was proud to be seen as forward. What is being forward but breaking the bounds that others have set for you, striding out ahead, taking a lead, carving out a path, making things happen? Let us enjoy ourselves and do all those things we want to do, and learn to ignore those who whisper behind our backs.

In any case you get used to whisperings behind the back if you are a Samaritan. The Jews refuse to recognize us as belonging to their race and religion. And yet we worship the same God, and we too are descended from Sarah and Abraham, from Rebecca and Isaac, from Rachel and Jacob,[4] as they are. True, we are more multi-cultural than they, because we have had a lot of immigration

and I see no reason to resist the idea that Jesus became close to some women who had chosen to have a large number of sexual partners. What I would resist is the labelling of such women as 'morally lax', and in my recounting of Photina's history I have attempted to tell the story through her eyes, in a way that I hope may arouse more sympathy than condemnation. In her own way, my character of Photina was quite a feminist, even if she did not think it beneath her dignity to make herself sexually attractive in men's eyes.

Many male commentators, however, have gone to town over her character. In a nineteenth-century commentary she has been described as 'a deeply fallen character', with an 'indifference to higher interests' and a 'roguish frivolity', and she was predictably stereotyped by that inaccurate description, 'a sort of Samaritan Magdalene' (John Peter Lange, *A Commentary on the Gospel According to John*, Edinburgh, 1872, p. 205). (For the mistaken idea that Mary Magdalene was a prostitute see note 16 on p. 119.) Even recently the Samaritan woman has been called 'a tramp' (see O'Day). Any such labelling could not be further from the attitude of Jesus himself to this woman.

4 Mention of the foremothers, along with the forefathers of the Jewish nation, is of course anachronistic: the women have come to be named only in recent feminist practice, and the traditional formulation was always 'Abraham, Isaac and Jacob'. Nonetheless I have included this linguistic innovation, partly because it is the sort of thing my character of Photina might have said if the idea had been suggested to her, and partly because I have considered it worthwhile to recall the female ancestors at some point in this book.

from Assyria.[5] We see that as a richness, but they say we are impure. Some 500 years ago we offered to help them build their temple, and they would not let us touch it.[6] They have always looked down on us, ever since, and worse than that, there have been a number of bloody incidents. People have been killed on both sides, and it only takes one life to be lost for a whole vendetta of revenge killings to be set up.[7]

I am proud to be a Samaritan, just as I am proud to be a woman. I am not going to think less of myself because those on the other side think they are better than me. If they look down on me, that is their problem. I am not offered the same rights as others, I am not going to cringe and beg or sit in a corner being humble. I shall make space for myself.

If you know anything about me you probably know me as the woman who had five husbands. I am sorry this should be considered the most interesting thing about me, but since that is what everyone wants to know about I had better clear it out of the way before we can move on to more substantial topics.

My first man was one of the group that I grew up with in my village – this was before I came to Sychar. I just decided who was the best of the bunch and I won him. It had not yet occurred to me to look beyond my immediate contemporaries, and I was well satisfied at the time. He was dark and straight-featured, athletic and even something of a dare-devil. I was the first of my friends to be married, and it felt wonderfully exciting and grown up. Sex

<hr>

5 2 Kings 17 recounts how the king of Assyria overran Samaria because, says the tradition, the people of Samaria had 'worshipped other gods and walked in the customs of the nations whom the Lord drove out before the people of Israel' (2 Kings 17:7–8). This happened in the eighth century BC, and Assyrian immigration began from then.

6 This was in the late sixth century BC when the Jews, returning from their exile in Babylonia, began to rebuild their temple. When the Samaritans were not permitted to assist they became difficult and tried to prevent the building work.

7 One such occurred shortly after the time of Jesus, in around AD 50, when some Samaritans murdered one Jewish pilgrim en route to Jerusalem for the Passover, and in return the Jews massacred the entire village of Gema (or Ginae).

was a thrilling discovery, to be explored night by night. Marriage was great, for the first few months. After that sex became a routine, and I began to feel dreadfully hemmed in. He had no aspirations beyond the village, and no ideas. I began to realize my intelligence went far beyond his, and I was bored out of my wits. I was growing, growing, in my mind and in my heart, and I left him far behind, like a childish plaything. I had made a bad mistake in marrying him, but I was so young and knew so little.

I fell in love with a man from another Samaritan town, whom I met when he passed through the village. He was a little older, had travelled more widely and had more experience of life. He too was a stunner to look at – with dark Persian looks[8] – but this time his conversation matched his features. It felt thrilling to be in his company, and my heart ached in the long gaps between his visits. Eventually the sequence of rare, illicit meetings punctuating a life of dreary frustration became unsustainable, and I went back with him to his home. But after a while he tired of my looks and turned to other women. His infidelity was a thorn, and the jealousy which I felt spurred me on to give him cause for jealousy too. That did not lead to a reconciliation, but rather to him divorcing me for adultery. The fact that he had been unfaithful first was never even mentioned.

I could hardly go back to my husband, and though my family were ashamed to take me in they were so happy to see me again that they relented. They hoped I would settle down now, but it was clear after a short while that there would be ongoing tensions at home about what we each considered reasonable behaviour, for having been a married woman twice over I was not prepared to go back to doing what Mummy and Daddy said. Equally soon I realized that I was in the early weeks of a pregnancy, which would make me even more of an embarrassment to them. The solution my family found was to scrape together enough to get me a little place of my own in the city of Sychar. There I would sink into a certain anonymity and yet at the same time they could feel they were providing for their grandchild. For me it was a perfect solution, since I was not afraid to live alone, and I brushed off the

8 Persians, as well as Medes, were among the foreign races who had intermarried with the Jews in Samaria.

spiteful and unfair murmurings in the village that I was being provided with the means to run a brothel.

By the time I gave birth to my daughter I had already furnished
my home with a new husband. Once again I was passionately in
love. Will I ever be able to live without passion? I hope I shall never
want to. But once again there were difficulties. My daughter's
arrival changed everything, for he felt pushed out by her. I tried
to make him see that he still had a role, but that a baby has needs
that are more urgent and cannot wait. I thought the situation
would sort itself out when the baby was no longer waking me by
night and requiring constant supervision by day. But by that time
we had a second child, and I had less time than ever before for this
rather selfish, demanding husband. I had hoped that since this was
his child he would resent it less, but that did not seem to happen.
In my heart I was thinking, 'Grow up and see what you can do to
help instead of acting like a child yourself.' Then I lost hope that
he would change, and began to hope instead that he would go,
because we were so unhappy together. But he sank further and
further into misery and resentment without having the strength to
do anything about it. I became pregnant again, and as I approached
my delivery date I knew I could not cope with a new baby unless
he went. I threw him out. It might seem cruel, but I knew it was
the best for him, as well as for me and the children.

I felt a great burden lifted when he went. Motherhood is hard
for anyone, and I was living away from my family, who would normally bustle round and take the fatigue away. But I preferred to
have independence even if it made for harder work. Free from the
shackles of a morose husband I found it easier to make friends now,
especially among those whom you might call the more worldly-
wise. My children provided me with a stable love that I had lacked
from my husbands. They were beautiful, and I knew their love for
me would last and they would not fail me.

I have seen a lot of women turn frumpy once they become
mothers, lose their sexual attractiveness and look plain and worn
and twice their age. I was determined that would never happen to
me. For my children's sake as well as my own I would stay young
and attractive, so they could be proud of me. What is more, I
wanted to find them a father, and I could never quite give up the
hope that there might be a good and reliable man in the world,
despite all my disappointments so far. To be honest, my shortage
of means meant I had no option but to be ready to accept a man
into my life again. I was fortunate to have somewhere to live, but
that was all I had. 'Pursue him. Make him support you', declared

my parents, about my third husband, father of my two younger children. But I could not take the risk of pursuing him for financial support: I might end up with him back!

So it was that husband four came to be welcomed into my home. He brought richness to life, in both a material and a social sense, and provided a little breathing space. But I was realistic about the future. 'I'll enjoy this while it lasts', I said to myself. If he was my fourth man, I must have been his tenth woman. And of course it did not last. He is the one I would really have liked to stay, but I always knew the odds were against it, and I did not let myself mourn too long.

Husband five was the worst disaster of all. He seemed a safe character, not a showy type, but quiet and intense. All went well for over a year, and I bore him my fourth child.[9] Then one day he hit me. Many women have been hit by their husbands of course, but there was a ferocity in the blow that put me on my guard. I said nothing to him, but to myself I said, 'If it ever happens again, if it ever happens again. . . .' A month later he lashed out again, knocking me to the floor and picking me up again by my hair before crashing my head against the wall.

Getting rid of a violent man is one of the most difficult and dangerous tasks that a woman can face. If I had not acted swiftly I would most likely have been sucked into a cycle of violence from which escape became impossible. There were others in Sychar like that – helpless victims, trying to soften the blows by their submission, forced to live a hidden life out of fear that any argument, any publicity, any outside plea for help, would earn them a beating from which they would never recover. Thank God that was not my style. My reputation was already so tarnished that I did not care what anyone said about me, for it is always the woman who is thought a liar and not the man. I laid plans long in advance, tipping off friends and neighbours, and asking them to turn up in force with all their acquaintances if there was any incident. Meanwhile I said nothing to him. Then when he was away one day I had the lock changed and bolts put on the windows. When he came back that night he stood outside and yelled and banged, but

---

9 We recall (see note 2 on p. 54 above) that according to legend Photina had two sons, Joseph and Victor. The legend does not say if she had daughters.

because a crowd gathered who knew exactly what the problem was, he could not touch me. He turned up every night for a week to make the same row, but my friends stood by me and came simply to be there and observe. In the end he gave up and went away, leaving nothing more behind him than a fifth child in my womb.

From that time on I knew it would be dangerous not to have a man in the house, for he could return at any time without warning, and so I took in friends and travellers and lodgers – anyone to keep the house occupied. Occasionally they slept in my bed, but that was not the usual pattern. From now on I was more wary of relationships, and felt I could never entrust myself to a man in marriage again.

This was the situation, then, on the day I am about to narrate. I had had a hard morning. The kids had been particularly difficult, coming home covered with dirt, with grazes all over their legs and their clothes torn. I swore at them, for I had not enough water both to clean them up and to cook the lunch. I dabbed at their cuts, but decided to leave the rest of them dirty until I went to the well in the cool of evening. Lunch was already late, but as I was beginning to prepare it I discovered the kids had used the cooking pots to make mud pies in. I would have to wash them carefully before we could have lunch – not just because of the purity laws[10] but so that we did not eat mud! – and that meant I would have to go to the well after all.

I cursed and grabbed the water jar and the bucket. At least the edge of anger drove me to overcome the weakness of hunger. My current companion lifted not a finger to help. I thought: why should it always be the woman who goes to the well? Life would be much less pressured if some of these jobs could be shared. But there is no point in saying anything to him: it would poison the air, and I will only have to go myself in the end anyway. And that would make lunch even later and me even crosser. 'Watch the children', I snapped, as I stormed out.

The streets were emptying and quietening, as people settled down to eat in their houses and courtyards. The shops were about to close, though I passed a group of Jews who were picking up

---

10 See Mark 7:4: 'there are also many other traditions that [the Pharisees and all the Jews] observe, the washing of cups, pots, and bronze kettles.'

some supplies. They were not having too easy a time of it, since no one is helpful to Jews. The well was outside the city, as it had been for centuries, ever since our holy ancestors, Jacob, Leah and Rachel,[11] bought a plot of land on the outskirts of Sychar and dug for water.[12] The walk would be onerous at this hour, because the sun was at its highest. The only consolation was that I would not have to queue at such a time. There would be nobody there.

As I passed the last house and set out towards the well I saw I was wrong. There was a man sitting on the wall of the well, looking tired.[13] I did not recognize him. He stayed there motionless as I approached, watching me. He insisted on staring at me fixedly while I fixed the bucket to the rope and let it down. I gave him a good few stares back, but he did not relax his gaze. I was irritated, but also intrigued. He might be tired but he had an intensity about him that was rather haunting. I positioned myself where I could keep him in my eye as I hauled up the bucket.

I lifted the bucket onto the edge of the well. It was heavy and dripping with good, clean water. The man looked at the water, and then at me. I could see how badly he wanted some. It occurred to me to offer him some, but a couple of things stopped me. Firstly,

11 Leah was Jacob's first wife, wedded to him by trickery. Rachel was always the one he loved, and she it was who became the mother of Joseph. In recognition of all women, the unloved as well as the loved, the plain as well as the beautiful, I have made Photina remember both wives here, and not just the favoured Rachel.

12 Sychar (or Shechem) was 'near the plot of ground that Jacob had given to his son Joseph. Jacob's well was there' (John 4:5–6). The well was regarded as sacred because of this ancestry. The basis for the tradition is found in three Old Testament texts: Genesis 33:18–20, in which Jacob camps before the city of Shechem, and buys the plot of land on which he had pitched his tent, and builds an altar to the God of Israel there; Genesis 48:22, in which Jacob gives to his son Joseph a mountain slope (Hebrew *shekem*, a play on the name of the city); and Joshua 24:32, in which the bones of Joseph were brought up from Egypt and buried at Shechem, in the portion of ground that Jacob had bought.

13 After a long introductory section I now pick up the story from John 4:4–42.

I was ravenous and did not want to make lunch any later. Secondly, in speaking to a strange man I would be playing yet again into the hands of those who said I was a flirt. Had I known at that moment that he was a Jew I would not even have considered it, since Jews will not share drinking vessels with Samaritans. I tilted the bucket so as to pour into the water jar.

'Give me a drink.' His voice was intimate, almost whispering, and it had a Galilean lilt. I froze. I knew I could get myself into another pickup situation – talking to a highly attractive foreigner out of sight of anyone else. It was a game I had played often, but did I really want to play it with a Jew? So instead of warmly granting him what he had asked for, as my outgoing nature would normally lead me to do, I drew back and played for time. Looking him hard in the face I pointed out that his advance to a woman who was a Samaritan was doubly indiscreet: I said, 'How is it that you, a Jew, ask a drink of me, a woman of Samaria?'[14] Meanwhile I sized him up.

We explored each other's faces with our eyes. When he spoke he left me more baffled than ever. At one level his words could be heard as a shameless, arrogant bid for my bed, for he said: 'If you knew the gift of God, and who it is that is saying to you, "Give me a drink", you would have asked him, and he would have given you living water.' And yet that did not fit. Apart from the fact that as a stranger he would have no idea of my reputation, there was something much deeper and more mysterious going on in his words that I did not understand. He spoke of God. Yet he did not sound like a religious maniac.

There was an electric charge in the air that was not unwelcome. Lunch or no lunch, I became aware that I was enjoying this conversation and wanted to prolong it. And I became aware that he was enjoying it as much as I. Like two wild cats at play, we were circling around each other, pretending to be enemies

14 'In the Mishnah and Talmuds', says Ben Witherington, 'there are various views recorded on whether Jews would have dealings with Samaritans and whether Samaritans and their possessions and land were unclean' (*Women in the Ministry of Jesus*, p. 166). He also points out that 'if this woman was living with a man other than her husband, she would be ritually unclean, yet Jesus shows no signs of maintaining the distinctions of clean and unclean' (p. 60).

while we were loving every minute of it.[15] And so I said, slightly tauntingly, 'Sir, you have no bucket, and the well is deep. Where do you get that living water? Are you greater than our ancestor Jacob, who gave us the well, and with his sons and his flocks drank from it?'

I was teasing him in several ways at once, and was pleased with my answer. Firstly, with a show of polite correctness ('Sir'), I was pretending to take his remark with innocent literalism and was asking where he would get the water from. Yet I knew as well as he that he was not talking of water from a well. What I did not know was what on earth he *was* talking about. Secondly, I was reminding him provocatively of our Samaritan right to the Jewish inheritance. Our well was given us by Jacob. He was *our* ancestor, and his sons and flocks made their home in this place, now *our* home. That was bound to annoy a Jew. Thirdly, I was challenging him to answer the question, 'Are you greater than Jacob?' What could he say to that but 'No'? And that would cut down to size his grand, cloudy phrases about living water and the gift of God. How are you going to meet that one, 'Sir'?

'Everyone', he said, 'who drinks of this water will be thirsty again.' I de-coded that to read, 'You may think you have the edge on me, because I am thirsty and you have the bucket, but that is no more than a superficial, temporary advantage.' After a slight pause he continued, with an intensity that overwhelmed me and made me feel a yawning hunger that was not for my lunch: 'But those who drink of the water that I will give them will never be thirsty. The water that I will give will become in them a spring of water gushing up to eternal life.'

What was there about this man that made me believe his crazy claims? With a gullibility I thought I had outgrown I found myself pouring my will into his, as I heard a tiny voice dragged out of me, saying, this time with no trace of sarcasm: 'Sir, give me this water, so that I may never be thirsty or have to keep coming here to draw water.'

What was I asking? I did not know that any more than I knew what he was talking about. But he had touched a nerve that was

---

15 There are, of course, many very different ways of reading this entire dialogue. This suggestion is only one of a whole range of different interpretations, and makes no claim to be the correct one.

raw inside me. To be free from coming here to draw water? If what he were saying were true even at face value alone it would be the most unimaginable liberation. Of all the burdens of my life, carrying water was the most onerous. Every morning and every evening. Quarter of an hour one way, twenty minutes at the well (often more if the queue was long), 25 minutes back with a massive weight on my head. That is two hours a day, before I can even begin to wash the clothes and to clean the house and to cook for the children. I can just about cope with it on a fine day when I am feeling fit and chirpy, but a woman's lot is to have to carry on in all weathers and in every state of health. Of course, none of my men, not one, has ever relieved me of the water-carrying, not once. To be free from that? Was that possible?

I did not know what the man was offering, but whatever it was I sensed it was a freedom no less than this. And so I pleaded, 'Give me this water', believing in some sense he could, though I could see full well with my own eyes he had no means of doing so.

Nor did he give me water. Was it to escape from a corner that he changed his tone and said, 'Go call your husband and come back'? Or was it to show that after all he would act with propriety and not chat up a woman who was alone? Whatever it was I was not going to be shaken off. I had absolutely no intention of going back home to bring back a man as my minder, no matter what the social expectations. If he wanted to talk to me he could get on with it, now, with me alone. So I said sulkily, 'I have no husband.'

His next remark knocked me sideways. 'You are right in saying, "I have no husband"; for you have had five husbands, and the one you have now is not your husband. What you have said is true.' Damn the man. This display of paranormal powers was a cheat. How can you carry on a conversation with someone who can magic a trump card out of thin air? So he had only told me to fetch my husband in order to give himself a chance to discomfort me. And I was to be typecast yet again as the loose woman. What the hell else did he know about me?

The brimming bucket was still tantalizingly waiting on the wall and he had had none of it. I turned my back on him and poured the water into my water jar, leaving none for him to drink. I was on the point of picking up my water jar and turning on my heel in disgust, but there was too much about the man that was intriguing for me to leave. And there was something about the way he had spoken of my past that lacked the customary tone of accusation. I searched his features again. What was in them? No, not superiority. Knowledge of me, certainly, and of a sort that made me afraid. And yet there seemed a kindness there that made that knowledge safe with him. I did not want his pity, any more than I wanted his criticism. But what I sensed there was neither criticism nor pity. It was respect.

I took the initiative again. 'Sir, I see that you are a prophet.' I hoped he would catch the slight sneer. And then I had second thoughts and hoped that he would miss it. 'Our ancestors worshipped on this mountain', I said, gesturing round at Mount Gerizim on the slopes of which we were standing. 'But *you* say' – I certainly put an edge into that 'you', which I rolled out to encompass the whole damn lot of them, 'but *you* say that the place where people must worship is in Jerusalem.' I was referring to the long-standing dispute between the temple in Jerusalem and our own temple, that we had built, with very considerable scriptural warrant,[16] on Mount Gerizim. Not content with banning us from their own temple, the Jews had destroyed our Mount Gerizim temple a little over a century ago.[17] Now we had only the site, without the building. Was I asking him what he thought? I did not intend to do him that favour. I intended to tell him how bigoted they all were.[18]

16   'When the Lord your God has brought you into the land that you are entering to occupy, you shall set the blessing on Mount Gerizim' (Deuteronomy 11:29). Some texts also read 'Mount Gerizim' for 'Mount Ebal' in Deuteronomy 27:4.

However, in the early second century BC, when the Jews were being persecuted by the Hellenistic ruler Antiochus Epiphanes, the Samaritans renamed their temple after Zeus Hellenios – no doubt a purely political move, but one which discredited them still further with the Jewish religious authorities. In similar fashion, the Samaritans hovered between claiming to be Jewish, and claiming not to be, according to expediency, or so reports the ancient historian Josephus (*Ant.* 11.340–342).

17   This happened in 128 BC.

18   According to nineteenth-century commentators, 'the caricaturing estimate of this personage represents her as everywhere frivolously bantering up to this point without intelligence or misgiving' (Lange, p. 212, referring to De Wette, Schweizer, Ebrard, Tholuck).

St John Chrysostom, however, gives a much more respectful

Yet again his response left me outmanoeuvred. In every one of his remarks since we began the conversation he had seized the advantage, and that annoyed me. And yet even as I sparred with him I felt myself drawn inexorably into the fascination of his presence and the magnetism of his personality. I thought I was wise to every trick of seduction, but he was winning me over at a level deeper than I had ever felt before. I felt he wanted me in a compelling way – far more than he wanted that drink of water – and I was thrilled by his tenacity.

'Woman', he said, and I almost felt he could have said 'Photina' if he had wanted, he seemed to know me so well, 'Woman, believe me, the hour is coming when you will worship God neither on this mountain nor in Jerusalem.' Great stuff, that, a grand appeal. But then came the barb. 'You worship what you do not know; we worship what we know, for salvation is from the Jews.' I would have risen to the attack then, for this typically Jewish piece of religious arrogance, but for the compelling sweetness of his next words, that

interpretation. He comments most favourably on the woman's interest in theological questions, contrasting her with the congregation to whom he was preaching. He sounds enchantingly modern as he complains that his contemporaries never read books, but play dice instead (we can almost hear him complaining that they watch television). Here is the passage:

'Let us, then, be ashamed and let us now blush. A woman who had five husbands, and was a Samaritan, manifested such deep interest in doctrine, and neither the time of day, nor her interest in anything else, nor any other thing diverted her from her quest for knowledge of such things. We, on the contrary, do not make inquiry about doctrine, but are indifferent and casual about everything. . . . Who of you, when at home, ever takes the Christian Book in his hands and goes through what is contained therein, and studies Scripture? No one would be able to say he does. However, we shall find that games and dice are in most houses; but never books, except in a few. And the latter have the same attitude as those who do not possess books, since they tie them up and store them away in chests all the time, and their whole interest in them lies in the fineness of the parchment and the beauty of the writing, not in reading them. . . . I hear no one priding himself because he knows their contents, but because he possesses one written in gold letters' (*Commentary on St John the Apostle and Evangelist*, Homily 32).

lifted me up with their vision and drove the thought of argument from my mind. He said, 'The hour is coming, in fact it is here already, when the true worshippers will worship God in spirit and truth. Those are the sort of worshippers God wants. God is spirit, and those who worship God must worship in spirit and truth.'

You can call it rhetorical. You can call it pretentious. You can call it the elegance of empty language and challenge me to tell you what it adds up to. But it won me over. Something deep inside me resonated with his words and a chord seemed to echo between us. Yes, it was true. Those who worship God must worship in spirit and truth. Oh to be able to do that, whatever it meant. To be able to worship God, in ways that did not trivialize and divide, that did not point to God here or there or anywhere, but opened up to the mystery of the eternal and the infinite. What temple, no matter how grand it was, could appear more than a worthless trinket in the eyes of God? What mountain, no matter how sanctified it was by past events, could be more than a grain of sand in the infinity of God's holiness? We struggle to find God by reverencing holy places, but all we are doing is trying to catch the wind in a box. We look inside, and there is nothing there. To be able to find God in spirit and truth. . . . What an invitation. God knows how to go about it, but talking to the man I felt I was closer to it.

I heard the man's words in silence, and let them reverberate in my mind. It was in a mumble, then, that I offered to the man my final attempt to challenge his certainties. 'I know that Messiah is coming', I said, 'It is Messiah who will tell us the truth about these things.' I would have said Taheb were I speaking to another Samaritan, and yet there was a sweetness in the gentle hiss of that word, unfamiliar upon my lips: Messiah.[19] Messiah is coming, the prophet whose words will be the words of God. Messiah is coming, and he will be ours as well as yours, and bring us an answer to all the wrongs we have suffered.

And the man said, 'I am.' Time stood still, as I wondered if I had heard him right. A heat haze hovered around us, insulating us from all other noises, as those shockingly sacred words hung in

19 The Samaritans called the Messiah they were expecting 'Taheb', and identified him with the prophet of Deuteronomy 18:15–19, where it is said, 'I will put my words in the mouth of the prophet, who shall speak to them everything that I command.'

the air between us. Then he said again, spelling it out gently and unmistakably for my distrustful ears, 'The one who is talking to you now is the Messiah. I am he.'

'I am', he had said. Those were the words heard by Moses when he stood before the burning bush on Mount Horeb and was told to take his shoes off. 'I am has sent me to you. The God of your ancestors has sent me to you.'[20] If the man had failed to vindicate the holiness of our mountain by his earlier words, he could hardly have hallowed it more by uttering that phrase. He had made Jacob's well a place of divine self-disclosure comparable to Mount Horeb.[21] Our ancestors had worshipped on this mountain. So what? The Messiah was now sitting before me on this mountain and talking to me.

And like God to Moses, he was sending me to the people with the message, for I could scarcely keep it to myself. I was afraid, I was excited, I was confused, and I barely noticed that the Jews I had passed earlier were suddenly arriving with much noise and to-do.[22] They started unwrapping a picnic as though they had no idea in whose presence they were standing. Food for the Messiah? He seemed above the mundane world of hunger, and I heard them urging him in disappointed tones to eat something. 'I have food to eat that you do not know about', he was saying.[23] Drink

20 The famous story of the burning bush is found in Exodus 3:14–15.

21 'In a spiritual sense all the dispensation of help to the Samaritans took place beside Jacob's spring' (Origen, *John*, Tome xiii.27).

22 'They were astonished that he was speaking with a woman, but no one said, "What do you want?" or, "Why are you speaking with her?"' (John 4:27). Contrary to the entire spirit of the episode so far, one of the early fathers (who is thought to be Clement) drew the perverse conclusion that Jesus thus 'set an example to all generations of abstaining from associating with women' (*Virgins*, ii.15).

23 John 4:32. Ben Witherington comments: 'With typical irony, the evangelist paints a contrast between the disciples who bring Jesus physical food that does not satisfy, while a woman brings Jesus his true spiritual food by helping him to complete God's work. Once

for the Messiah? He almost seemed to have forgotten his original plea of thirst, but in any case he could have his fill now for I turned and fled leaving my water jar and bucket behind with him.

In the city everyone was at lunch, but that did not deter me. I began knocking at the doors of all the people I knew, quite unapologetic for disturbing their midday meal.[24] 'I have just been talking to a man who told me my life story', I said, 'You don't think he could be the Messiah, do you?' I knew damn well he was, of course, but I would have put them off if I had appeared too naive. 'Come and meet him', I urged subtly, 'then you can advise me if you think he is genuine.'[25]

again the pattern of reversal of expectations and of expected male–female roles becomes apparent' (*Women in the Ministry of Jesus*, p. 62).

24 Teresa of Avila writes of her high esteem for the Samaritan woman who became witness to Christ, as follows: 'I have just remembered some thoughts which I have often had about that holy woman of Samaria, who must have been affected in this way. So well had she understood the words of the Lord in her heart that she left the Lord Himself so that she might profit and benefit the people of her village. This is an excellent example of what I am saying. As a reward for this great charity of hers she earned the credence of her neighbours and was able to witness the great good which Our Lord did in that village. This, I think, must be one of the greatest comforts on earth – I mean, to see good coming to souls through one's own agency. It is then, I think, that one eats the most delicious fruit of these flowers. Happy are they to whom the Lord grants these favours and strictly are they bound to serve Him. This woman, in her Divine inebriation, went crying aloud through the streets. To me the astonishing thing is that they should have believed a woman – and she cannot have been a woman of much consequence, as she was going to fetch water. Great humility she certainly had; for, when the Lord told her of her sins, she was not annoyed (as people are nowadays – they find it difficult to stand home truths) but told Him that He must be a prophet. In the end, her word was believed; and merely on account of what she had said, great crowds flocked from the city to the Lord' (*Conceptions of the Love of God*, chapter VII, trans. E. Allison Peers).

25 'Come and see a man who told me everything I have ever done! He cannot be the Messiah, can he?' (John 4:29).

Who wants to go out in the midday sun and in the middle of their lunch, even on the enticement of meeting a prophet? They would come later, they said, when they had finished their meal and had a rest. So I had to urge haste. 'He'll have gone', I cried, 'he's just about to go now, when he and his friends have finished their picnic.' 'We cannot come now', they said, 'we are sorry but it is lunchtime.' A wonderful array of cooking smells met me in house after house, but I had lost all thought of food. I did not waste time, but ran on to the next house where I knew people. I had to knock up five households before I found anyone prepared to come, and I pointed them in the direction of the well while I went to rouse some more. I told you I could attract a following! What I achieved on an empty stomach!

I must have spent an hour knocking on doors, before I finally went back home to collect my own kids. When we all returned to the well, the man was holding court now to quite a large crowd. This time I could sit back and enjoy it, as others did the talking. I felt more and more proud of the man, who I now learned was called Jesus, and who came from Nazareth. The men from the city were trying to put hard questions to him, just as I had done, and I watched with great satisfaction as their expressions changed from incredulity to admiration. His Jewish friends were looking impatient, and from time to time they tried to draw him away to continue their journey, but Jesus made it clear he was not going to budge while so many people were interested in what he had to say.

We were out there for hours. We were all sitting on the ground by now, while Jesus sat on the edge of the well and talked to us

John Chrysostom is impressed by the woman's preaching technique: 'See how prudently she spoke. She did not say: "Come and see the Christ", but she, too, attracted the people with a gradual approach similar to that by which Christ had drawn her on. "Come and see a man", she said, "who has told me all that I have ever done." She was not ashamed to say: "who has told me all that I have ever done". . . .

'She did not say, "Come and believe", but "Come and see", which was less difficult than the other, and attracted them more strongly. Do you see the wisdom of the woman? Indeed, she knew, she knew clearly that, having once tasted that fountain, they would believe the same truths as she' (*Commentary on John*, Homily 34).

about God. How pious it sounds! But the real thing is not pious: there is no one who can fail to be drawn by the real touch of God. After a while people arrived who had said earlier they were in the middle of lunch. And after that there began to arrive those who wanted to draw water. As they drew it they became engrossed in what they were hearing, so they sat down with their full water jars and the group got bigger and bigger. Then their friends and families came out to look for them, and the crowd got bigger still.

So there we all were, with the plop and the splash of the water forming a background to the discussion, and the children running around on the edge of the group, and sometimes coming closer for a few minutes, drawn by his strong and compelling voice, before running around happily again. And there were Jesus' Jewish friends, sitting looking blank on the outskirts, as awkward as ever Jews looked in Samaria, and from time to time they stood up to gesture to Jesus impatiently that the sun was getting lower in the sky.

Eventually it was clear that if they did not go now they would have to spend the night in our city, and the offers of hospitality came up thick and fast, as everyone wanted to be the one to have Jesus stay with them overnight. He listened as the offers came in, and then thanked us graciously saying that, yes, he would like to stay. But each person's offer he accepted on behalf of one or other of his travelling companions – and there were close on two dozen of them [26] – so suddenly we found our Samaritan city was to give free hospitality to a whole crowd of Jews, which was rather an unexpected feeling, but not at all an unpleasant one in the glow of that moment.

And then Jesus announced that he himself would stay with the citizen who had first befriended him, [27] and everyone's eyes looked

26   As argued in the chapter on Mary of Magdala (note 24 on p. 124) it seems that Jesus was customarily accompanied by a group of female travelling companions as well as the twelve male disciples.

27   This is in the spirit of the teaching that apostles should remain with their initial host: 'Whatever town or village you enter, find out who in it is worthy, and stay there until you leave' (Matthew 10:11; see also Mark 6:10 and Luke 9:4; 10:7).

with amazement and envy – and in many cases horror! – at me. And so Jesus spent that night in my house, and the next night too, before his party moved on again in the direction of Galilee. When they left I found I could not walk more than a few steps down the street before someone would come up to me and say, 'It is no longer because of what you said that we believe in him. We have heard him for ourselves. And we are quite sure that he is indeed the Messiah.'[28]

You might think that was the end of the story. But it was only the beginning. Just think for a moment, and you will see why. How many times did Jesus journey from Galilee to Jerusalem and back again? You cannot remember them all, and neither can I, but in those brief three years he made the journey a fair number of times. And how do you get from Galilee to Jerusalem? Why, only through Samaria. And where did he stay on his journey through Samaria? Why, with me of course. And so I kept in close touch with Jesus through all those years, right up to his final journey.

I learnt a lot from him in all those meetings, every time I opened my door to him and brought him into my home. One thing he taught me was the powerful symbolism of light. 'I am the light of the world', he would tell me, 'Whoever follows me will never walk in darkness but will have the light of life.'[29] Then it was with

28 John 4:42. Rachel Conrad Wahlberg draws attention to John Calvin's slighting of the woman's testimony: 'Calvin can't resist saying in his *Commentaries* that the Samaritans "appear to boast that they have now a stronger foundation than a woman's tongue, which is, for the most part, light and trivial".' Calvin had also suggested that Jesus had only brought up the subject of the woman's husbands 'in order to repress the woman's talkativeness', and that, when Photina roused the city to come and meet Jesus, 'she merely does the office of a trumpet or bell to invite others to come to Christ'. This last comment aptly draws from Conrad Wahlberg the riposte, 'Merely? That is true preaching' (*Jesus According to a Woman*, Paulist, 1975; rev. edn 1986, pp. 90, 91, 95).

29 John 8:12. Jesus as light of the world is a favourite theme of the fourth gospel: see John 1:4–9; 3:19–21; 9:5; 12:35–36, 46. The next phrase, however, is based on the imagery of light as used in Matthew, where it is the disciples rather than Jesus who are called 'the light of the world', and likened to a city on a hill that cannot be hid (Matthew 5:14). See also Matthew 6:22–23 and Luke 8:16–17; 11:33–36.

great affection that he turned to call me his little light. 'You too, Photina, because you are a little light, must raise high your lamp to lead the way for others. Look how Sychar stands out for miles, because it is built on the slopes of Mount Gerizim. A city built on a hill cannot be hid. In the same way, hold your light up high and do not be afraid of what others say of you.'

And so I learned that I had a role and a dignity, and though I continued to be marked by others as 'the one who had five husbands', something had changed in me. I never wanted to marry again, for I had found resources within myself that I did not know I had. In that sense there really was a spring within me, gushing up to eternal life, as Jesus had promised. You could call it self-sufficiency, but it was not quite that, for I was more than ever aware how dependent I was on the grace of God. I lived in gratitude for what I had, rather than in craving need of what I lacked. I was never going to be a 'respectable' woman, and I had no desire to be seen as such.

And yet I had won respect of a somewhat unusual kind through the privileged place Jesus had given me in his life and work. Everyone in the city knew it was I who had brought them the news of Jesus. They also knew it was my house he stayed in, and they never paid him the indignity of suggesting he needed a chaperone. People usually seemed ready to accept special rules for Jesus, and some of this flexibility inevitably stretched to me, to my advantage. I was no longer typecast, for I no longer fitted any type.

I also learned to have close men friends who did not share my bed. Now that Jesus was my most intimate and esteemed friend, it would have felt disloyal to give anyone else a physical place that he did not have. I am not pretending I did not miss the bodily comfort I had enjoyed. But something in me had lost the taste for second-rate sex and would rather do without.

The more I learned of Jesus the more my self-respect grew. I learned, for example, that he never – but *never* – told anyone he was the Messiah. And yet he had told me. He had told a woman, and he had told a Samaritan, and I would never forget those words echoing in the summer silence when I spoke to him of the Messiah. 'I am. The one who is talking to you now is the Messiah. I am he.' I, who had known so much intimacy, had never known an intimacy so deep. Nor had Jesus shared that privilege with anyone else, man or woman, not in Samaria, not in Galilee, not in Judaea, not before me, and not after me either. How right I had been to feel that something special was happening to both of us that day, as though we were each holding the ends of a quivering string which was almost inaudibly emitting its hum between us.

Not only did he never tell anyone else he was the Messiah, but whenever anyone recognized it for themselves he enjoined them to silence. Being the Messiah was his secret,[30] and it is obvious why. He would be killed for it. And he was killed for it. It was only because Samaria was seen as such a dump, on the edge of no man's land, that he could let the knowledge get out freely there. I had in effect told the whole city that he was the Messiah, and he never suggested that I should keep the news to myself.

By not telling me to keep it quiet he had in fact sent me out to spread the news. And that is one reason why that day on Mount Gerizim I had felt a bond with Moses on Mount Horeb, for he too was sent out. The message for the Israelites through Moses was: 'I am has sent me to you.' And the message for the people of Sychar, through me, could also be expressed: 'I am has sent me to you.' Sychar was the first place where Jesus allowed this news to be spread, and I was the first to be sent out to spread it. In other words, I was the first apostle.[31]

30 The messianic secret is a constant theme of the gospels, especially of Mark. See Mark 1:25, 34, 44; 3:12; 5:43; 7:36; 8:26, 30; 9:9 (and parallel texts in Matthew and Luke); see also Matthew 9:30; 10:27. The theme of the messianic secret is in some ways less marked in John, but echoes of it can be found in Jesus' escape from the crowds who wanted to make him king (John 6:15); in Jesus' failure to answer the crowds' dispute on precisely the topic of his messiahship (John 7:40–43); and in Jesus' refusal to give a straight answer to Pilate's question, 'Are you the king of the Jews?' (John 18:33–37). A clear reason for the messianic secret is given in John 9:22: 'Anyone who confessed Jesus to be the Messiah would be put out of the synagogue.'

31 Origen grudgingly calls her an 'apostle'. He comments that, though she was 'a female easily deceived', yet Jesus 'uses this woman as an apostle to the people in the city, having kindled her so greatly through his words'. He continues: 'Here a woman preaches Christ to the Samaritans; at the end of the gospels the woman who had seen the Saviour before all tells his resurrection to the apostles' (John, Tome xiii.26–27).

   Without explicitly giving her the title of 'apostle', John Chrysostom compares her work of evangelization favourably with that of

Do not get me wrong. I am stating a fact, not claiming any merit for it. With my life the one thing I had no illusions about was my own weakness and the many mistakes I had fallen into. No, it was no virtue of mine that made me the first apostle. Indeed the very idea is laughable.

∽

the twelve: 'As far as she could, she herself did as the Apostles had done; nay, with even more alacrity than they, for they left their nets after being called, while she of her own accord, with no summons, left her water-jar and did the work of an evangelist with excited elation as a result of her joy.

'She called not one only and then a second, as had Andrew and Philip, but having roused the entire city, even though it included so great a throng, she brought it all to him' (*Commentary on John*, Homily 34).

Even Augustine recognizes that what she was doing was 'preaching the gospel', and he urges, 'Let them who would preach the gospel learn; let them throw away their water-pot at the well' (*On the Gospel of John*, Tract XV. 30).

Eva Catafygiotu Topping (see note 2 on p. 54) says that 'it was a woman who brought Jesus his first converts', and she continues: 'In Greek sermons written between the fourth and fourteenth centuries, the Samaritan woman is compared to the male disciples and apostles and found to be their superior. During this same period many hymns were composed to honour the woman at the well. The poet of an elaborate sixth-century hymn calls her "wise", "holy", "faithful" and "god-bearing". With one voice Greek hymn writers sing the praises of the woman who, when she received the water of eternal life, rushed to share it with others. In more than a few hymns the Samaritan woman is herself glorified as a "spring of living water". In time she was canonized by the Eastern Orthodox Church and enrolled among her saints. Her cult spread throughout the Eastern Mediterranean world, and reached as far west as Spain' (*Holy Mothers of Orthodoxy*, p. 57).

Elisabeth Moltmann-Wendel recognizes that the woman of Samaria 'became the first apostle to the gentiles' (*The Women Around Jesus*, p. 23). But given the early occurrence of this incident in only the fourth chapter of John's gospel, we can say she was the first apostle altogether. Though the twelve were called early in Jesus' ministry, they do not seem to have been sent out on preaching missions until considerably later (Matthew 10:5, Mark 6:7, Luke 9:2; 10:1), and their preaching of Jesus as Messiah seems to belong to the post-resurrection era.

The point maybe is that God does things which are laughable. A Samaritan the first apostle? What a joke. A woman the first apostle? How absurd. A divorced woman? Five times divorced? And still in an irregular relationship?[32] If that is the sort of ambassador the Messiah chooses, then what kind of Messiah is this?

And you know the answer as well as I do. A Messiah who knows that everyone is as much of a fool and a sinner as I am. A Messiah before whom no one can put on airs and graces. A Messiah who lifts up the despised, and passes over the self-satisfied. A Messiah who brings into the reign of God even the Samaritans, even the gentiles, even those with the wrong colour skin and the languages that no one knows or cares about. A Messiah who frees us from the stranglehold of human estimation, and who looses the tongues of the dumb, yes, even the tongues of women.

32 Photina is three times marginalized, for her race, her sex and her marital status. Nor was she well off, for Teresa of Avila recognizes – see note 24 on p. 70 above – that 'she cannot have been a woman of much consequence, as she was going to fetch water'. In a similar way modern feminism recognizes the plight of those women today who are three times marginalized, especially those who are poor and black as well as female.

THE STORY OF
MARTHA

OF BETHANY
WHO WELCOMED AN ADOPTED BROTHER AND
REDISCOVERED A DEAD ONE

My name is Martha and I live in Bethany with my sister, Mary, and my brother, Lazarus.[1] Mary is a couple of years younger than me, and rather different in temperament. Where I am efficient and organized, she is dreamy and forgetful; I keep my head screwed on, while she lets her heart run away with her; without me the home would fall apart; without her it would be reduced to boredom.[2] Lazarus is our younger brother, and I suppose I still think of him as our 'little' brother, even though he has been fully grown for years![3] But I always take special care of him, especially since the time when I thought we had lost him forever, as I will recount shortly.

We love having people to stay with us. Since Bethany is

1 According to legend, Martha, Mary and Lazarus came to be expelled from Palestine for their faith, were put on a raft and arrived in France, where they spread the gospel. From the twelfth century onwards Martha was evoked as a figure for a new women's consciousness, especially in the south of France. She is also associated in iconography with a tamed dragon, as a symbol of evil and of the old order. I shall not pursue any of these lines in this chapter, but shall confine myself to the scriptural material.

2 E. Stauffer describes the difference between the sisters like this: 'Martha appears resolute, energetic, ready of tongue, used to giving orders, as eager to make suggestions as to reprove . . . Mary is hesitant, slow, quiet, easily moved, obedient, devoted' (*Jesus and His Story*, trans. R. and C. Winston, Alfred A. Knopf, New York, 1974, pp. 223–4).

3 Of the three siblings, Lazarus remains in the gospel accounts a shadowy figure, while it is Martha and Mary who are more prominent. Bethany is even called 'the village of Mary and her sister Martha' (John 11:1).

only a couple of miles east of Jerusalem, it is a very pleasant place for those who like to be just a little bit outside the bustle of Jerusalem and do not mind walking in. We are fortunate to have a room we can set aside as a guest room: it means a lot to us to have a house open to the stranger, for the bible has always taught us to 'love the stranger, for you were strangers in the land of Egypt' (Deuteronomy 10:19).

And what riches our visitors bring! There is nothing we love more than meeting new people and hearing their experiences, and sitting for hours in the courtyard over a meal – eating, drinking and talking, with many friends from the village enjoying the company of our guests. I love cooking, and it is great to have people to cook for – like a musician having an audience! What could be a greater pleasure than sitting over a lovely meal? When we have guests it is not a self-indulgence but a work of hospitality. It is our favourite form of relaxation. But it has not always been like that. Some years ago we made a special friend, who taught us two great lessons. One was the beauty of hospitality: he was the first to find a habitual niche within our home. The other was the importance of relaxing and enjoying our guests: before that I used to find the demands of hospitality turning into a burden and a cause of anxiety.

Jesus was outstandingly special to us, but I also can say with total honesty that we were equally special to him.[4] He did not really have a home, unless it was ours, since the time when he left his mother's house in Galilee. We were like his adopted family – we all got on so happily and naturally together, and our house was one place where he could really relax. He came very often indeed over a period of three years, and in that time we always kept our spare room free for him, so that he could always feel he had a home and family ready to receive him. Usually he turned up with a whole crowd of friends – there were twelve men and a number of women who travelled with him[5] – and we found lodging for all of them

4 Ben Witherington (in *Women in the Ministry of Jesus*, p. 108) points out that Martha and Mary of Bethany are the only women mentioned by name as being the object of Jesus' love: 'Jesus loved Martha and her sister and Lazarus' (John 11:5).

5 For the women travelling companions, see note 24 on p. 124, in the chapter on Mary of Magdala.

around the village. It was quite an invasion – but such a joyful and stimulating one that Bethany seemed a very sleepy and empty place when they had gone.

After his companions went to their lodgings, Jesus would be alone with us in our house, and would speak to us very frankly about his feelings and fears. Many, many times the four of us would sit up late at night talking, and experiencing that warm sense of satisfaction when a scattered family is brought together again.

As time went by that sense of warm reunion became more and more fragile and more and more precious, as there were plots against Jesus' life and any visit to the Jerusalem area was fraught with danger. There was a very special quality to those evenings as we came closer to his end. He would stay with us on his way into Jerusalem, knowing that he was walking into a sea of knives. Two or three times I wondered if this would be the last occasion I would see him alive. There was a particular tenderness between us in those dark nights, because of our shared, unspoken fear. We never tried to persuade him against going – we understood how strong a sense he had of his vocation. We did not want to make it more difficult for him by playing the role of tempter, suggesting that his work was not worth the risk of his life. Rather, we felt privileged to be his last staging post, as it were, on what might be his final journey. But inside us . . . well you can imagine. It was like a family kissing a soldier son goodbye as he went off to war.

But first I will tell you of a memory from earlier and happier times – quite soon after we came to know Jesus.[6] In fact it was the first time he had dined with us. In any case I invited some friends from the village as well as all of Jesus' travelling companions, and I did my best to make a marvellous meal for that big crowd. I wanted so much for it to go well. I began early in the morning, buying the best ingredients and making preparations – throwing away anything that had got slightly spoiled in the cooking and starting again – and all day long I was in such a rush to get everything ready in time. I had to go back to the shops when I found I was out of lemons, and then again when I began to worry whether we had enough fresh bread. Lazarus was out all that day, so he did nothing at all – he was just due to turn up in the evening

6 This story follows Luke 10:38–42. The other gospel references to Martha and Mary of Bethany are found in John, chapters 11 and 12.

and find it all ready. Mary did a few things to help, but she did not care about making it extra-special. She just did what she considered essential and then lost interest. I was irritated seeing her gaze out of the window in her dreamy way while I was slogging my guts out and getting increasingly panicky about whether the meal would go right.

I laid the tables outside in the courtyard, and put an oil lamp on each. I put out our best dishes and coloured cloths, and made sure that the plants were well watered and free of any fading leaves. I swept and washed the floors, and set little vases of flowers on the tables. It was like preparing for a king to come to supper. Well, it was preparing for a king to come to supper. I was worried and stressed, and kept going over all the details in my mind, afraid I would forget something. And the more I worked, the crosser I got with that lazy sister, who could see how I was sweating and just sat around. 'Can't you do something to help?' I said, 'Can't you see that I'm preparing for Jesus to come?' And Mary replied, 'I'm preparing for him to come too.' 'No you're not', I said, 'you're sitting around doing nothing.' 'I'm preparing for him in my own way', she said.

Jesus arrived with his gang, and one by one all the other guests turned up, and I was rushing to and fro making sure they all had drinks. Mary said, 'Why don't you just leave the cups and the water and wine jars on the side table and let them serve themselves?' But I could see they were so busy being introduced to each other and chatting that it would be an age before they got themselves served. And then I had little dishes of olives to hand around. The pity was that I wanted to meet Jesus and hear what he had to say, but there was not much chance. I had to get everyone seated, and then bring the first course, and by the time I had served[7] the last person it

7 Because the Greek word used in the gospel for Martha's work is *diakonia* (Luke 10:40), some scholars, such as Elisabeth Schüssler Fiorenza, suggest that the story reflects a tension in the community between ministering in the diaconate (in an early-Church sense) and listening to the Word. The early-Church concept of the diaconate is introduced in the Acts of the Apostles 6:6, where it is presented as the charge of more practical charitable works and 'serving tables', as contrasted with the 'prayer and ministry of the Word' undertaken by the twelve. Acts is also written by Luke, the

was time to bring in the second course to those who had already finished, and then I had to collect all the plates and wash them and bring them back, as we did not have enough for everyone to have clean plates for the fruit salad I had made. 'Why don't you let them eat the dessert off the same plates?' said Mary, as I bustled past her. 'Because they are covered in gravy', I answered crossly. Mary said, 'Can't they clean them with a bit of bread?' I gave her a withering look.

As I washed the dishes inside the house I felt my anger and frustration like a knot inside me. I so much wanted to hear what Jesus had to say. Here he was in my own home and I had not had time to listen to a single story he was telling. I felt so excluded, because I was the only one to miss out on the conversation. From outside I could hear laughter and happy voices, and again and again people falling silent as Jesus' deeper voice took over, but I could not catch the words. It was not fair.

I was angry with Mary, because she was not doing a half share of the work. She was sitting out there listening to Jesus when she should have been carrying in the dishes. And I was angry with Lazarus, because he was not lending a hand either. He even seemed quite oblivious of the problem, though as one of the hosts he should have felt responsible. And more than that I was angry with men

author of the present story, so a good case can be made for the parallel.

'However', she writes, 'it must not be overlooked that the "good portion" chosen by Mary is not the *diakonia* of the Word: it is not the preaching but rather the listening to the word. The characterization of Mary as a listening disciple corresponds to the narrative's interests in playing down the leadership role of women' (*But She Said: Feminist Practices of Biblical Interpretation*, Beacon Press, Boston, 1992, p. 65). For Mary's silence see also note 11 on p. 85.

I have not pursued the notion of *diakonia* here, but it is worth noting that some interesting work has been done recently on the meaning of *diakonia*, especially by John N. Collins in *Diakonia: Reinterpreting the Ancient Sources* (Oxford University Press, 1992). He suggests that *diakonia* is not confined to serving tables, but can also refer to the going-between of representatives and ambassadors; its tone therefore is not so much one of subservience as of responsibility.

See also note 10 on p. 84 for further interpretations of what Martha and Mary represent.

in general. Men did nothing. They sat there like princes while you buzzed to and fro attending to their needs. And then they looked down on you as a woman, because you knew less than them. You knew less because you were washing dishes instead of having the chance to listen and learn. And you were expected to wash dishes because you knew less and people felt you had less to offer to the conversation. It was a vicious circle. Of the guests out there, not a single man had even bothered to pass his plate along the table for stacking, let alone moved an inch to bring the dishes out to the kitchen. Not a single one.

And as I faced my feelings of anger and resentment I knew I was even angry with Jesus, because he too was a man, and he too had failed to clear away his plate, and he was at the very centre of the group that was enjoying itself and excluding me. If he was such a just prophet as he was made out to be, then he ought to see the injustice. He ought to do something about it, and not just sit there talking to everyone else as though I did not exist.

I returned to the courtyard with the clean plates and the fruit salad: just taking that lot out involved six journeys – three for the stacks of plates, and three for the three big bowls of dessert. As I served it I was so burning with indignation I could not even concentrate on what Jesus was saying – although for once I was in earshot. Wonderful phrases seeped through – there was something about a man living in a pigsty, a quarrel between relatives, and then a moving declaration of sharing at the end, 'Son, you are always with me, and all that I have is yours.' Something in me wanted that sharing – and did not know how to get it.[8]

Suddenly people were saying that the evening had turned chilly. Some went home, and some moved inside and sat in an

8 A student of Elisabeth Schüssler Fiorenza, Jean Young, wrote: 'If the one thing that will help Martha with her anxieties and troubles is a shift in her view of herself and her role, the repercussions will be told around the world. She will no longer speak through a male authority figure, she will no longer put up with a group who expect to be waited on, she will take the good portion as she wants it and demand it as it is forthcoming. She will find a relationship to God Herself that fits for her which may well include both preaching and serving at table. She will reclaim her friendship with Jesus. She will raise hell.'

attentive huddle around Jesus, and Mary was right there at his feet,[9] looking up at him, her eyes glowing with admiration. I did not go with them, I went back outside and cleared the tables.[10] As I carried things in I hissed, 'Mary. Come on.' She looked awkward for a moment, but she did not move, she turned her face back to Jesus. I was so jealous.

I burst out to Jesus, interrupting him, 'Do you not care that my sister has left me to do all the work by myself? Tell her to help me.' There was an embarrassed silence, and I flushed red. Jesus held out a hand to me, and drew me into the circle, and without

9 Ben Witherington says: 'The use of the phrase "to sit at the feet of" in 10:39 is significant since there is evidence that this is a technical formula meaning "to be a disciple of".' He adds: 'For a rabbi to come into a woman's house and teach her specifically is unheard of' (*Women in the Ministry of Jesus*, p. 101).

10 The ancient, traditional interpretation of the Martha and Mary story is of the tension between the active life (Martha) and the contemplative life (Mary), with the contemplative life emerging as superior on the grounds that Mary had 'chosen the better part'. But St Teresa of Avila tried to restore the balance by saying both approaches were essential: 'This, my sisters, I should like us to strive to attain: we should desire and engage in prayer, not for our enjoyment, but for the sake of acquiring this strength which fits us for service. . . . Believe me, Martha and Mary must work together when they offer the Lord lodging, and must have him ever with them, and they must not entertain him badly and give him nothing to eat. And how can Mary give him anything, seated as she is at his feet, unless her sister helps her?' (*The Interior Castle*, VII, iv).

The story has also been seen as reflecting the contrast between justification by works (Martha) and justification by faith (Mary).

My own interpretation, however, is to see it as reflecting the tension experienced by almost every woman between the time-consuming demands of catering (shopping, cooking, laying meals, clearing them up) and the desire for education (in the broadest sense of the word). Every woman has a Martha and a Mary within her, locked in conflict, as she struggles to free time from her domestic commitments in order to work with her mind or with her artistic abilities. The message of Jesus appears to be: if you have to decide between guilt over neglecting your house and guilt over neglecting your brain, give priority to your brain.

letting go he said gently, 'Martha, Martha, you are worried.' 'Yes', I nodded. 'You are distracted by many things.' 'Yes, yes', I nodded. 'But there is only one thing that is really needed.' I wondered silently, 'What's that?' but he did not say. Instead he said, 'Mary has chosen the better part, which will not be taken away from her.'

I did not know whether to smile or cry. I did not get my way – but then it was not really that I wanted both Mary and myself to miss the conversation, but that I wanted neither of us to miss it. Jesus drew me to sit down next to him, moving away one of his twelve. And the good thing was that I now felt free to leave the dishes. I felt free to do what I really wanted, which was to sit by Jesus and listen to him and be warmed by his peaceful presence. I felt Jesus was saying to me, 'This talk is for you too, Martha, though you are a woman, and though you feel others see your place as the kitchen. But to me you are not a kitchen maid. You have as much right as any man to talk about God and morality and the purpose of life and all those other big philosophical questions. You belong here.'[11]

11 According to Jane Schaberg, Luke presents Mary's role in listening to Jesus as purely passive, involving listening but no talking: 'The disciples and apostles in Luke learn often in dialogues (e.g., 5:1–11; 8:4–15; 9:10–11), but Mary is silent. Her attitude is that of a disciple, but she is not a disciple. She is only an audience. What she has heard and learned at the Lord's feet is private; it does not instruct and shape the whole community' (*Women's Bible Commentary*, p. 289).

Elisabeth Schüssler Fiorenza also takes exception to Mary's passivity. 'Mary, who receives positive approval, is the *silent* woman, whereas Martha, who argues in her own interest, is *silenced*. Those who praise Mary's extraordinary role as a disciple generally overlook the fact that Mary's discipleship only includes listening but not proclamation' (*But She Said*, p. 62). She takes this line even though she has noticed that sitting at the feet as a disciple is not seen as a demeaning position by the writer of Luke/Acts: 'Just as Paul was the Pharisaic student of Gamaliel (Acts 22:3), so Mary is a disciple of Jesus, dedicated to listening to his word' (p. 59).

Whether or not Luke presents Mary as passive, if we look for the role of Martha and Mary behind John's gospel we find evidence that both women were proclaimers and interpreters of the gospel. Martha makes a classic credal statement (John 11:27). Mary performs the verbally silent but symbolic, eloquent action of anointing Jesus as the Christ (John 12:1–8), which is explored in the next chapter.

Through my resentment and anxieties I felt affirmed. I thought that exceptionally, since we had such a very interesting guest, I could just this once leave the dishes till the morning. What I would regret was missing out on Jesus, not having a pile of work waiting to face me in the morning. And I listened spellbound, as Jesus had permitted me to do. I felt I was present at a historic moment, and that the minutes were like grains of gold dust. It was as though all the anxieties and distortions of my life were dissolving, and the compelling power of Jesus' words was shining through – like cloud cover melting to let the brilliance of the sun pour down. Was that what Jesus meant about the 'one thing needed'?[12] I felt that love and peace were so strong in the room around Jesus, that it would bear me up for the rest of my life.

And in a sense it has, for ever since I have been able to relax and enjoy having guests – and we have had many more of them. Jesus' words did not solve my external problem – too much housework, with others not taking their fair share.[13] But his words did solve my internal problem – anxiety and resentment about it. And that in its turn has made a small contribution over the years to my external problem, for people are more willing to join with me in what I am doing when they can see I am appreciating joining them in what they are doing.

I have told you how our life with Jesus began, and now I will tell you how it drew towards its end. Jesus, as I have told you, loved us. Everyone knew he loved us – each one of us differently, because

12 An alternative reading of Luke 10:42 is 'few things are necessary, or only one', which has been taken to mean that a meal does not need many items. But I prefer to see the 'one thing needed' as that singleness or purity of heart (cf. Matthew 5:8) in the love of God that allows all lesser concerns to find their appropriate place.

13 The objective problems of woman's double life are considerable and can never be simply dismissed with an exhortation not to fuss. In the words of Schüssler Fiorenza, a text such as this 'blames women for too much business and simultaneously advocates women's "double role" as "super women". Women ought to be not only good disciples but also good hostesses, not only good ministers but also good housewives, not only well-paid professionals but also glamorous lovers' (But She Said, p. 69).

we were so different. Lazarus, then barely more than a youth, was like a younger brother to Jesus – someone he watched over with pride as he developed. He would do anything for Lazarus.

Lazarus fell ill.[14] He lay in bed all day with a high fever, and Mary and I thought it was just a bout of 'flu which would pass. (I was my new relaxed, unanxious self, remember! Or at least trying to be.) But each day he got worse. He stopped eating. He sweated till his sheets were sopping. He trembled and his mind began to wander. The doctor told us to sit up all night with him, as his condition was dangerous. Mary and I drew up a rota of people to sit at the bedside, and a list of other things to be done. And top of the list was to send a message to Jesus. He had healed so many people that we had no doubt at all he could heal Lazarus. We knew where he was, although he was in semi-hiding. He had escaped from Jerusalem when people began to take up stones to stone him with, and he had crossed the Jordan to the place where John used to baptize.[15] We sent a friend, who returned to tell us the message had been given. As soon as we knew that, our worries left us and we looked forward with confident joy to the healing. Jesus would arrive any moment, we felt sure.

He did not arrive that night, nor was he here by the next morning. We had shopping to do, but delayed it as we did not want to be out when Jesus came. Lazarus was heaving and shivering in a way that would have terrified us if we had not believed that salvation was a few minutes away. By late afternoon I told Mary I would have to go out and shop as the provisions were urgent. I rushed home and asked eagerly 'Is he here yet?' But I could see from Mary's face that he was not.

The next night was more worrying. I took the first watch, but

14 The story we are about to explore, from John 11, is traditionally called 'The raising of Lazarus', but Gail R. O'Day points out that this is something of a misnomer: 'Of the 44 verses that constitute this story, only seven of them take place at Lazarus's tomb (11:38–44). The miracle of the raising of Lazarus is the climax of this story, but it is not its centre. The story centres on the conversations Jesus has as he travels to Lazarus's tomb.' His conversation partners are Martha and Mary (*Women's Bible Commentary*, p. 297).

15 This is recounted in John 10:31 and 40.

when Mary came to relieve me I said I would stay as I could not sleep anyhow. I was listening all the time with one ear to Lazarus' erratic breathing, and with the other for the rustle of stones or faint knock that might indicate Jesus was here. We did not hear the rustle of stones all night long, and after three o'clock we did not hear Lazarus' breathing either.

We buried him in the evening. In that summer heat you cannot afford to keep a dead body unburied for long. And so the corpse of Lazarus was wrapped in white cloths and laid in the family cave. I thought my heart would break when the door was sealed: it was such a final symbol. There was no hope now that the eyelids might flutter again, or the skin begin to warm. Our grief and our sense of betrayal were equally strong. We were surrounded by dozens of people, many of whom came out from Jerusalem to be with us in our time of bereavement. The days were intolerably long, and the hours when we were able to find relief in sleep were far too short.

Four days later one of our neighbours slipped in and said quietly to Mary and me, 'Jesus is coming.' Both Mary and I felt a stab of anger, but Mary was the more furious, I think. She refused to respond at all – she just went on staring out of the window as though she had not heard. I got up straightaway and went to meet him.

I saw him coming from far away, surrounded by his usual mob, along the edge of the cornfields. I walked towards him, and he walked towards me, and it was a good ten minutes before we met. The yellow corn was swaying, and the sun was beating down, and with every step I was wondering what I would say. Anger now was giving way to a hurt incomprehension. I suppose I felt in doubt of his love for us.

We said nothing as we came close, but let our eyes guide us together until we were face to face. Then we both stopped and just looked at each other – hurt meeting love. I kept reasonably calm and controlled, because I am that sort of person, but I knew my mouth was dry and my head was buzzing with tiredness and grief. And I said, keeping my voice as steady as I could: 'If you had been here, my brother would not have died.'[16] And there was such

16 On this remark, which was made in identical form by Mary also (John 11:21, 32), Elisabeth Moltmann-Wendel comments: 'For Martha, however, this remark is a springboard, the introduction to a passionate conversation about faith. Martha is not "a woman" who "keeps

concern in Jesus' face that I then dropped my eyes and added, 'But even now I know that God will give you whatever you ask of him.' I do not know what I was hoping for, but I felt the need to express some kind of faith in him.

All this time the twelve were keeping as still and silent as if they had been drilled soldiers, rather than the rabble they usually were. It was after all the first confirmation they had had that Lazarus had indeed died from his illness, and they took the news with solemnity, and even, I suspect, with something of my own incomprehension.

Jesus said to me, very gently, very tenderly, 'Your brother will rise again.' I lifted my head and looked into the distance behind him and said, hesitantly, 'I know that he will rise again, in the resurrection, on the last day.' And I felt like adding, though I did not, 'So what for that? What good is that to me now?' In the distance I could see birds, flying and swooping and weaving through the air. And I thought how the immortal soul of Lazarus, which would rise at the last day, was no more comfort to me now than one of those birds, circling and dipping in the distant sky.

Jesus said, 'I am the resurrection and the life. Those who believe in me, even though they die, will live, and everyone who lives and believes in me will never die. Do you believe this?' What was he saying? Were these words to comfort a bereaved woman? What sort of life, or death, was this? Was he reminding me that my grief was self-concerned, and that Lazarus was not the loser for passing from this world? Lazarus certainly believed in Jesus. I did not really know why Jesus was saying these things, but against all reason there was a strange comfort in them, and I felt he was asking me for a sign of faith. We had after all lost faith in Jesus in rather a major way. There was a need to reaffirm it. I did not understand his behaviour, or what he was trying to tell me, but I wanted to reach out and recover our former trusting relationship, in an unconditional way.

The words that came out took me by surprise, not because I

silence" in the community. She does not leave theology to the theologians. She carries on a vigorous debate. She does not cry, she does not cast herself at Jesus' feet, she does not give in. She struggles with God as Job did. She charges Jesus with failure' (*The Women Around Jesus*, p. 24).

did not know I believed them, but because it was not done to say such things. If I had never said anything like this before, no one else had done so either.[17] It was the kind of admission which could lose Jesus his life. But we were in an exceptional situation, and I felt it right to say it – to say it all – and to risk looking foolish for it. It was the sort of thing that a woman could look extremely foolish for saying. It was like saying for the first time, 'I love you.'

Jesus had ended, 'Do you believe this?' I answered, 'Yes. I believe that you are the Messiah, the Son of God, the one coming into the world.'[18]

And that was such a big thing to do – to be the first person to make a public profession of faith that Jesus was the Messiah –

17 Martha is presumably unaware of the private conversation between Jesus and his disciples, when Peter made a similar profession of faith, 'You are the Messiah, the son of the living God', since Jesus warned them to talk of it to no one (Matthew 16:16).

18 All this conversation comes from John 11:21–27. Martha's profession of faith is 'the central Christological confession of this Gospel, of Jesus as the Christ' (Jane Schaberg, *Women's Bible Commentary*, p. 289). It is of parallel importance, to Peter's profession of faith, which appears in Matthew, Mark and Luke, but not in John. 'Christ' is the Greek translation of the Hebrew 'Messiah'.

   Lilia Sebastiani calls these words: 'a solemn profession of messianic faith in Jesus, which actually equals the confession of Peter, and possibly exceeds it for its heroic character – because it was made not only at the moment of greatest pain, but when Jesus, as Messiah, seems to have disappointed all the hope placed in him, and even as a friend has shown himself uncaring' (*Tra/Sfigurazione*, Queriniana, Brescia, 1992, p. 35).

   Elisabeth Moltmann-Wendel comments: 'For the early Church, to confess Christ in this way was the mark of an apostle . . . We must conclude from this story and this confession that Martha is also a leading personality, like the apostles in the early Church. She was a tenacious, wise, combative, competent, emancipated woman with many practical responsibilities in the community. She had a strong sense of reality ("the body is already rotting"!) and was good at organization: "the teacher is here and is calling you", she says to Mary, although he hasn't said a word. Still, we should not imagine her on a bishop's throne or with apostolic status, but as a normal housewife or mistress of the house' (*The Women Around Jesus*, p. 25).

that I then turned round, leaving Jesus standing in the cornfield, and I went back to the house. I took Mary aside where no one else could hear and said to her, 'Jesus is here. He wants to see you.' And this time she did respond. She ran quickly out of the house towards the cornfield, so that I hastened to follow her. And several others followed us, who must have thought she was running to the tomb and wanted to accompany her there in her grief. So they too hurried after Mary, following not to the tomb but to the cornfield.

Mary is an emotional woman whose public displays sometimes embarrass me. And on this occasion she threw herself on the ground in front of Jesus, howling. She practically screamed at him, 'If you had been here, my brother would not have died.' The words were exactly the same as mine, but the whole manner of saying them could not have been more different. I had restrained myself and shown respect and reaffirmed my faith; Mary was throwing herself on the ground and crying hysterically. I was ashamed, but Jesus loves her, with her personality which is so different from mine, and he was visibly moved. When I kept my calm, he kept his, and when Mary lost hers, he lost his. Suddenly I was hearing Jesus cry out with great distress, 'Where have you laid him?' So our little group, which had now fully caught up, told him to come and see.

And Jesus wept as we led him. The Messiah wept. The Son of God wept. Our friends nudged each other as we walked to the tomb and said, 'See how much he loved Lazarus.' But there was more to his tears than that. I think they were tears of sorrow for the hurt he had caused us – Mary and me. And indeed he had. Well might he weep. I also think they were tears of distress – not for Lazarus, because he already knew what he was going to do – but for the cycle of death that embraces this world.[19] We were not the only family to lose a brother. The work of salvation was so massive, so endless. And there would be another death, very, very soon.

19 Gail R. O'Day writes: 'Jesus' tears may be a sign of his love for this family, as some in the crowd suppose (11:36), but that is not all they signify. Jesus weeps also because of the destructive power of death that is still at work in the world. Once again one sees the intersection of the intimate and the cosmic: the pain of this family reminds Jesus of the pain of the world' (Women's Bible Commentary, pp. 298–9).

When we reached the cave Jesus said through his tears, 'Take away the stone.' I thought this was crazy, since the body had been in there decomposing in the summer heat for four days. It did not occur to Mary to point this out, so I thought I had better do so. Perhaps Jesus did not know how long Lazarus had been dead. So I said: 'There is already a stench because he has been dead four days.' Jesus said firmly, as though to remind me that I had just made a famous declaration of faith and must not show any doubts now, 'Did I not tell you that if you believed, you would see the glory of God?' Then I told the men to move the stone.

Jesus stood before the open door – there was not in fact a stench – and he raised his arms and eyes in prayer to God. 'Thank you for hearing me', he prayed, 'I knew that you always hear me, but I have said this for the sake of the crowd standing here, so that they may believe that you sent me.' Then, to everyone's amazement, he shouted into the tomb, 'Lazarus, come out!' Then he waited. And to their utter astonishment Lazarus did come out.

My brother came out stumbling, because he could hardly move his legs for the binding cloths, and because he had a piece of cloth covering his face and could not see where he was going. And his jaw was tied up with a bandage so he could not talk either. If we had not been so flabbergasted I suppose we might have found it comical. But we really were dumbfounded and frozen to the spot, and it was Jesus who told us to pull ourselves together. 'Unbind him', he said, 'let him go free.'

When Lazarus was untied he emerged as fit as ever, if a little dazed. 'What happened?' we asked him, but we were not much the wiser. 'I don't know', he said, 'I was woken up by shouting, and I recognized Jesus' voice, so I thought I would get up and follow it. I found it was difficult to move. At first I wondered if that was because I was in a dream, but as my sensations became more and more real I realized I must be stumbling out of my own tomb.'

Mary took one of his arms, and I took the other, and Jesus linked with Mary's other arm, as she was still very exhausted and hysterical, and we all went home. We made quite a procession. We had a party all day and all night long, with music and feasting and dancing. And this time I did not cook a thing – it was all done by friends and neighbours. I was overwhelmed with gratitude towards everyone in sight, and most of all of course towards Jesus. 'It is God you should thank', he said, 'you saw God's glory, didn't you?' When dawn broke we sent everyone home and went to bed, and all four of us slept, lulled by happiness, for hours and hours and hours.

I would like that to be the end of the story, but as you know it was not. Lazarus' rising was Jesus' dying, for as more people came to believe in Jesus through this miracle, so the priests plotted more frantically to put an end to him. That was the tragic irony with Jesus. When people recognized him as Messiah his death was sealed. So he became a different sort of Messiah from the one we expected. Jesus only lived a few weeks after the raising of my brother. We regained one brother, only to lose another. Maybe that is why Jesus put us through all that agony, so that we would be better prepared for losing him.

My sister Mary was the first to understand and to proclaim, in her own inimitable way, that Jesus was a Messiah who was to die. And at the same time she was saying a huge and extravagant 'thank you' for Lazarus. She will tell you the story herself.

THE STORY OF
M A R Y

OF BETHANY
WHO ANOINTED THE CHRIST FOR HIS DEATH

My name is Mary. I live in Bethany, and I am the sister of Martha. I think she has already told you quite a bit about me and about the times Jesus spent with our family. She has probably told you how emotional and irresponsible I am. It is a reputation I do not much like, but there is not much I can do about it.[1] And no doubt you will think the same thing, by the time I have finished telling you about the most important event of my life with him.

It was even more than that: it was the most important thing that happened between Jesus and anyone – whether they be man or woman. It was so important that Jesus said straightaway, at the time, that wherever the gospel would be proclaimed throughout the world, this incident would be told in my memory.[2] He saw it as

1 The emotionalism (e.g. John 11:33, 12:3) of Mary of Bethany (so often confused in the past with Mary of Magdala) and her dreamy taciturnity (e.g. Luke 10:39) is not always appreciated, even by other women. Indeed, feminists can feel that this type of woman fits too easily the glove of male fantasy. Elisabeth Moltmann-Wendel, for example, reacts rather sharply against her: 'From Mary we have only one sentence, which Martha had already uttered: "Lord if you had been here, my brother would not have died." Otherwise there is nothing but tears, falling down at Jesus' feet, sitting at Jesus' feet, anointing his feet. Many women today find this kind of behaviour offensive rather than attractive. . . . To be gentle, to be lovely, to be able to fall on one's knees is not necessarily a sign of strong faith. The New Testament, and above all John's story of the raising of Lazarus, had made this plain. Rudolf Bultmann, at any rate, has seen clearly that John wanted to use Mary to depict the first stage of faith. "She does not have Martha's certainty" ' (*The Women Around Jesus*, pp. 54–5). But see also note 29 on p. 108 below.

2 Matthew 26:13 and Mark 14:9. It is reasonable to identify the anointing in Matthew 26:6–13 and Mark 14:3–9 with the anointing in

John 12:1–8, even though the name of the woman is not given in Matthew and Mark. In all three cases the anointing forms the initial event of the passion cycle (as Bach recognized by beginning his *St Matthew Passion* with it). And in all three cases it takes place at Bethany (though there is disagreement as to whose house it takes place in – Simon the leper's according to Matthew and Mark; Lazarus' according to John).

What is more arguable is whether Luke's account of the anointing in Luke 7:36–50 is the same incident, occurring as it does much earlier in the gospel, although Luke follows Matthew and Mark in placing the event in the house of a man called Simon, and in speaking of an alabaster jar. Luke's account differs in that the woman is called 'a sinner', which is generally taken to mean a prostitute. It is unlikely that Mary of Bethany was 'a sinner' in this sense. In my view the similarities outweigh the differences, and it is likely that it is a single incident that is variously recorded, according to different people's memories. But this conclusion is not universally accepted. The notes to the New Jerusalem Bible, for example, say of Luke's account, 'This episode is not the same as the anointing of the Lord's head at Bethany, Mt 26:6–13 and par., although versions of that incident may well have influenced some of the details of the narrative here.' Augustine has a quaint hypothesis: 'My theory is that it was the same Mary who did this deed on two separate occasions' (*The Harmony of the Gospels*, bk 2, ch. 79).

There is nowadays almost universal dislike for the ancient tradition of the Church, much represented in iconography, that the anointing was performed by Mary Magdalene. Though not one of the gospels connects her with the anointing, the theory arose from identifying the woman called Mary (in John) with the repentant prostitute (in Luke), and then in turn connecting the composite figure with the disciple, Mary Magdalene, from whom seven demons had gone out (Luke 8:2). The assumption was that someone who had had seven demons must have led a very wicked life and must have a great deal to thank Jesus for.

'The identification', says Lilia Sebastiani, 'was at first sporadic and uncertain or only tentatively suggested, but it became finally accepted and proclaimed as true by Pope Gregory the Great. Gregory's great authority and his organization of the liturgy, among other areas, settled the matter, and it was practically beyond discussion in the West for fourteen or fifteen centuries. The Eastern Church, on the other hand, has always distinguished the three figures from the gospels.'

By the end of the nineteenth century, the distinction between the three women was accepted in Protestant circles, but 'Catholic scholars only began to get to a clear idea of the distinction of the "three Marys" in the first decades of the twentieth century' and this has 'still not been accepted fully in homiletics, still less in popular thinking' (*Tra/Sfigurazione*, pp. 11–12).

a part of the essential core of his message of salvation – a part so central that the gospel could not be proclaimed without it. Unfortunately those who transmitted the gospel later became increasingly unfaithful to him in this.[3]

Jesus, as you know, raised my brother Lazarus from the tomb and gave him back to us, his family. It was a dramatic miracle, well attested by many onlookers, and memorable beyond words, as Lazarus stumbled out in his grave-clothes. It was truly a manifestation of God's greatness – what Jesus himself called 'the glory of God'. We celebrated all night, and beyond, and our thanks to Jesus knew no end. All this is obvious.

The identification is now rejected for the following reasons: (1) although all the gospels know of Mary Magdalene because they all refer to her elsewhere, not one of them says she performed the anointing; (2) there is no reason at all to take seven demons to imply prostitution or even wickedness – it is more scriptural to take it as a reference to illness; and (3) seeing the woman of the anointing as a prostitute is a way of undermining the importance of the act and the dignity of the woman who performed it.

3 The fact that the anointing is recorded (in one form or another) in all four gospels, is itself an enormous tribute to its centrality. The only other events of which this can be said are the baptism (just about, in John), the feeding of the five thousand, the cleansing of the temple and the passion cycle itself (of which the anointing properly forms an integral part). But already in the gospels there is beginning to be some slippage from the authentic tradition: Luke misses the significance of the story in reducing it to simply a tale of repentance and thanksgiving; and though Matthew and Mark record the saying 'wherever the gospel is proclaimed in the whole world, what she has done will be told in remembrance of her', they then absurdly omit her name. This omission called forth the now famous first paragraph of Elisabeth Schüssler Fiorenza's book, In Memory of Her:

'In the passion account of Mark's gospel three disciples figure prominently: on the one hand, two of the twelve – Judas who betrays Jesus and Peter who denies him – and on the other, the unnamed woman who anoints Jesus. But while the stories of Judas and Peter are engraved in the memory of Christians, the story of the woman is virtually forgotten. Although Jesus pronounces

After the raising, I spent a long time in silent thought and in prayer about how I should respond to this miracle which had changed my life. I wanted to give Jesus the biggest gift I could. What can you give to a man like Jesus? I wanted to give him everything I had – but what use are money and possessions to him? He had given away all his money and possessions. I

∽

in Mark: "And truly I say to you, wherever the gospel is preached in the whole world, what she has done will be told in memory of her" (14:9), the woman's prophetic sign-action did not become a part of the gospel knowledge of Christians. Even her name is lost to us. Wherever the gospel is proclaimed and the eucharist celebrated another story is told: the story of the apostle who betrayed Jesus. The name of the betrayer is remembered, but the name of the faithful disciple is forgotten because she was a woman.'

Stephen Barton, however, argues, not entirely convincingly, that: '. . . from the point of view of narrative criticism . . . her anonymity is critical. First, it allows her to be placed alongside the many other anonymous characters in Mark who are exemplary in some way or other. Think of the woman with the haemorrhage, the daughter of Jairus, the Syrophoenician woman and her daughter, the children brought to Jesus by their mothers for his blessing, the "many women" who were present at the cross, and the unidentified centurion. Second, the woman's anonymity, together with the anonymity of her accusers (14:4a), constitute an invitation to the reader to identify with one or other of the two parties' (Stephen C. Barton, 'Mark as narrative: the story of the anointing woman, Mk 14:3–9', The Expository Times, vol. 102, no. 8, May 1991, pp. 230ff.).

In later Church tradition the anointing was increasingly ignored. It is not celebrated liturgically in the approach to Good Friday, as is, for example, the entry into Jerusalem – on Palm Sunday – or the Last Supper – on Maundy Thursday. It is rarely read as a Sunday gospel. Given the extraordinary theological significance of the anointing, this omission is flabbergasting. No other explanation has yet been adduced for its neglect, other than Schüssler Fiorenza's theory that because it is a story about a woman it was therefore assumed to be of no particular importance.

wanted to give him the service of my whole life – but that is easily said. Hundreds of people had said that, and what did it mean in the end? I needed to encapsulate that gift in some way – to find some symbolic way in which I could give him myself and everything I had – like at a marriage. Within a day of my brother's return to life I had come to that firm conclusion, and I felt it was right, though I had not yet found the right symbol.

But within the next two or three days I began to discover that, by resurrecting my brother, Jesus had been even more generous than I had realized. The news was coming back to us of how the authorities in Jerusalem were taking it. One might have thought that, with such an incredible but well-witnessed miracle, they would finally be convinced that the hand of God was with Jesus. Instead, they showed that they despised the works of God, and were more intent on protecting their exclusive claim to be God's spokesmen than on looking for the truth. The rumours coming back to us were that, precisely because the miracle was such a big one with so many witnesses, they were more determined than ever to have Jesus killed, and were from that moment putting into action a plan for his arrest and execution.

My thoughts and prayers now had a new element: how could I show, both that I gave Jesus everything, and that I recognized that he had exchanged his life for that of Lazarus? How could I show that I believed he was the Messiah – and that I knew he was a Messiah who was about to be murdered?

What is more, time was running out. Jesus could be arrested any day.

I did not talk about this with Martha: she would not have understood. Martha knew he was the Messiah, all right. She had been brave enough to say so, while everyone else kept quiet because they were too embarrassed about looking foolish. And we had often talked about the danger surrounding Jesus. We had even asked each other more than once if we would ever see him again. But right now Martha was so happy about Lazarus being alive that she was discounting the threats to Jesus. She thought, as everyone else did, that because he had revealed his power as Messiah so dramatically he had shown that he too would escape death. How did I know he was really going to die? It was simple: Jesus had said so. He had several times told his closest friends – and we of course were among his very closest friends – that he was going to Jerusalem to fall into the hands of the chief priests, to be mocked and spat on and scourged, and to be put to death.[4] I cannot think why no one believed it other than me. And yet I knew he could still be the Messiah, because he also said he would rise from the dead on the third day.

And now my gesture had to be one that showed: that I loved him and poured out my thanks to him with the gift of all I had; that I recognized he was about to die, as a result of what he had done for me;[5] and that even through this death, he was the Messiah. It was quite an undertaking.

I went into Jerusalem, to the temple, and I prayed for guidance. Then I came out and I wandered round the streets, cocooned in my thoughts amid the hubbub of people. I walked down the street that had the most expensive shops in the whole country, and I gazed at their displays. There were fine silks and gold ornaments, but they were not quite right for the king who was on the side of the poor.

One shop had jars of ointment, for anointing the bodies of the dead. I stopped, and looked more closely. Here was something that could be a sign of faith in his death. There were various oils and unguents, beginning at one denarius for a small jar, and rising in price from there. The finest – and most expensive – ointment was spikenard.[6] I had smelled it once, and knew there was nothing to match it. They were selling it in alabaster jars,[7] and I looked at the different sizes – there was one at 30 denarii, one at 50, and one at 100. And then there was the most beautiful, big jar: the label said there was a pound's weight of ointment there, and it cost 300 denarii. Three hundred denarii! Why, it would take a labourer 300 days to earn enough to pay for that! You could say that alabaster iar of pure nard was worth nearly a year of my life.

~~~

4 He says this in Luke 9:22 and 18:31–34.

5 Foremost in Mary's mind would have been the raising of her brother, Lazarus, from the tomb.

6 Spikenard was made from the roots and hairy stem of an aromatic herb native to India.

7 Pliny tells us that 'unguents keep best in alabaster containers' (*Natural History*, 13.3.19; trans. H. Rackham, Loeb Classical Library, IV, 1945, p. 108).

My heart skipped a few beats and I walked quickly on. An argument was raging inside me. One side said, 'Don't be a bloody fool, Mary. Don't lose your head. Don't be absurd.' The other side said, 'Only a year of your life? Not quite a year? What is that? Didn't you say you wanted to give Jesus all the years of your life?' The first side said, 'Look here, Mary, you know perfectly well that 300 denarii is your entire savings. You wouldn't have a penny left for your old age, or for giving to charity, or for emergencies.' The other side said, 'Remember how Jesus taught you not to store things up for the future, but to be as poor as a lily of the field.' The first side said, 'Buy a smaller jar, for heaven's sake, it's only supposed to be symbolic.' The other side said, 'How can you give Jesus second best, especially at such a moment, when he is about to die?'

I didn't breathe a word to Martha or Lazarus, though they sensed I was brooding and tried to cheer me up and chivvy me along. But I would not be drawn, and would not be bounced out of my preoccupation. I had a big decision to make.

By the next morning it was made. I dug up the box of my savings (it was buried for safety in a hidden place), went back to Jerusalem, and came back with the large and fragile jar. I was terrified I would drop it on the way home, especially since I was so embarrassed about it I was carrying it underneath my cloak. I hid it in my room, and went and helped Martha in the kitchen – much more cheerful now it was too late to change my mind.

What I now had to wait for was Jesus' next visit, hoping there would be a next visit. Supposing we never saw him again? His end must be very close. Please God may Jesus come before it is too late.

In those days of waiting – they were few days, but they passed slowly – I prepared myself for what I had committed myself to do. I prayed and I read the scriptures. And the more I read, the more awesome I found my task.

I discovered, to my amazement, that anointing could be a most sacred act, hedged around with warnings against sacrilege if anyone took it into their own hands to anoint the wrong person. God instructed Moses to take the finest spices and make of them a sacred anointing oil. Then Moses was told to anoint Aaron and his sons, so that by this act of consecration they would serve God as priests. The anointing oil was holy, and was not to be poured on any ordinary person, for the one on whose head the anointing oil was poured was exalted above his fellows. Anyone who did so or who tried to imitate this religious rite of anointing was to be cut off from the people.[8]

By solemnly anointing Jesus for his forthcoming sacrifice, with the finest, purest, most fragrant oil, would I not be sharing in this religious act? What Moses did to Aaron, would I not be doing to Jesus? Would I not be anointing him, and ordaining him, and consecrating him, so that he might serve God as a priest?[9] But was not my act an even more sacred act, for an even greater high priest, who would make an even more holy offering? Surely if the priests at Jerusalem had any inkling of what I was doing they would cast me out with terrible anger.

I read on, with growing alarm. I discovered that anointing was a sign not only of priesthood, but also of kingship. I read how God revealed to Samuel that he was to anoint Saul to be king of Israel, to save the people from their suffering. Samuel woke Saul at the break of dawn and brought him alone into the deserted streets. He took a vial of oil and poured it on his head, and kissed him. And then the Spirit of God entered Saul, so that he prophesied.[10] So was I to pour the oil on Jesus' head? And to kiss him? And would he then be empowered by God's Spirit to carry out his mission as king of Israel, and to save the people from their suffering?

I read also how Samuel anointed David to be king, in the place of Saul. He took a horn of oil and anointed David in the presence of his brothers, and the Spirit of God came mightily upon David from that day forward.[11] Was I to play the role of

⁂

8   These instructions are found in Exodus 30:22–33 and Leviticus 21:10.

9   Moses is told to take Aaron and his sons and 'anoint them, and ordain them, and consecrate them, so that they may serve me as priests' (Exodus 28:41).

10   This story is recounted in 1 Samuel 9:15 – 10:13.

11   1 Samuel 16:12–13. Other instances of the anointing of kings are given in 2 Samuel 5:3; 19:10; 1 Kings 1:39; 2 Kings 9:6; 11:12; 23:30.
    The coming of the Spirit after anointing is a theme continued in the New Testament. Jesus is anointed 'with the Holy Spirit and with power' (Acts 10:38), and Christian believers, who have received the gift of the Spirit are also said to be 'anointed' by God (2 Corinthians 1:21–22).

Samuel?[12] He had been unique in the history of our people, for he was a prophet who became judge over Israel – the highest political and spiritual authority in the land and a precursor of the monarch. Was I, a woman, to anoint someone greater than David? Was I to consecrate the Messiah, the anointed one of God?[13]

I read still further. I read how the prophet Elijah was commissioned by God to anoint kings and to anoint Elisha as prophet in his place.[14] So anointing had a threefold significance. I was to anoint Jesus as priest, king and prophet. And I was to follow in the footsteps of not only Moses and Samuel, but Elijah too. And

12 In connection with the woman's prophetic role, and in consideration of the fact that it is virtually universally accepted that Luke had Mark's text to work from, Jane Schaberg comments bluntly on Luke's suppression of the 'female prophet': 'Given the emphatic nature of Mark 14:9, Luke's editing displays real arrogance. Politically, prophetically, what she has done will *not* be told in memory of her' (*Women's Bible Commentary*, p. 286).

Sadly but perhaps predictably, it is Luke's theologically impoverished version, in which the anointing woman is not a prophet but a sinner, which most people remember, and which has been depicted in art, to the virtual exclusion of the other three accounts.

13 'Christ', which means 'the anointed one', is the Greek translation of the Hebrew 'Messiah'. Jesus is anointed by God – 'your holy servant Jesus, whom you anointed' (Acts 4:27) – though it is the hand of Mary that pours the oil.

The anointing by Mary has been almost totally ignored, and theologians, if pressed about when Jesus was anointed, fall back on the baptism, when water was poured on his head and the Spirit descended like a dove. (This may be the interpretation implied by Acts 10:37–38.) Without wishing in any way to detract from the importance of the baptism, which opened Jesus' public ministry, it must be pointed out that the baptism was only an anointing in a very metaphorical sense. The great saving cycle of his death and resurrection was initiated by the literal anointing, which was at Bethany. This is further demonstrated by the fact that Jesus enters Jerusalem as king as his immediate next act in John's gospel (John 12:12–19). Neither the baptism nor the anointing made Jesus something he was not before, but rather revealed who he was, and set his saving mission in motion.

14 Elisha is anointed as prophet in 1 Kings 19:16.

then I remembered that our scribes taught us that Elijah must come again, before the great day of the Messiah.[15]

I was humbled, frightened, and overwhelmed. But I could not back off now, for I had bought the alabaster jar for 300 denarii. All I could do was hope that Jesus never came again, so that I would never have the chance to anoint him. That way the decision would be taken out of my hands.

But Jesus did come. Six days before the Passover[16] he came to dinner with us.[17] It was to be now or never. I knew he would

15 In the last verses of Malachi, which is the last book of the Old Testament, it is written that 'I will send you the prophet Elijah before the great and terrible day of the Lord comes' (Malachi 4:5). This tradition is referred to in Matthew 17:10 (Mark 9:11), when the disciples question Jesus about the scribes' teaching on the return of Elijah before the day of messianic salvation. The more familiar interpretation of the prophecy is to identify John the Baptist with Elijah (Matthew 11:14), on the grounds that he turned 'the hearts of parents to their children, and the hearts of children to their parents' (Malachi 4:6 and Luke 1:17). The Baptist, however, denies he is Elijah (John 1:21). But another instance of the return of Elijah is the appearance of the prophet himself at the transfiguration (Matthew 17:3, Mark 9:4, Luke 9:30). Finally, Mary of Bethany also plays an Elijah-like role by virtue of her prophetic sign-action of anointing, which comes more immediately before 'the great and terrible day of the Lord'. She is the 'destined Elijah' who, in the words of Ecclesiasticus 48:8, 'anointed kings . . . and prophets'.

16 Matthew and Mark date this supper as two days before the Passover, which is even more dramatic. I have followed the fourth gospel here, simply because I have also followed John in naming Mary as the woman.

17 According to Matthew and Mark, the anointing takes place in the house of a leper, which has dramatic power in the reversal of sacred space. Just as the holy sacrifice is offered on the polluted ground of Calvary – an execution site for criminals – so the holy anointing takes place not in the temple or at the tent of meeting where Aaron was anointed (Exodus 29:4–7), nor even in the ordinary secular space of a normal home (John), but in the polluted space of a leper's house. 'Lepers were, for obvious reasons, social outcasts, contact with whom brought ritual impurity as well as the danger of contagion. To share

never come again. Lazarus was there, surrounded by happy friends congratulating Jesus on this living, breathing evidence of his power. Martha served the meal and presided over the occasion,[18] with dignity, gratitude and pride. I was the only person at table to be quiet and moody. Jesus was certainly not moody, though I did feel he had an air of sadness, as though he was carrying a burden.

∞

a meal with a leper in his home was certainly an unusual situation. Most commentators assume that Simon's leprosy has been cured, although the text does not say so' (Mary Ann Tolbert, *Women's Bible Commentary*, p. 270). 'This inversion of spatial symbols of holiness is intended to express an inversion in the idea of holiness itself and the world-view of which it is an expression. As we know from chapter 7 [of Mark], purity is no longer outer cleanness threatened by contagion. Rather, it is a matter of what "comes from within" (7:23). This allows boundaries established to protect from contagion to be subverted. Jesus becomes the one who liberates all who find themselves on the wrong side of the boundaries and who find the laws of ritual purity oppressive. Such people include women and lepers. So it is not at all coincidental that the anointing of Jesus as king is performed by a woman in the house of a leper' (Stephen C. Barton, 'Mark as narrative: the story of the anointing woman, Mk 14:3–9', *The Expository Times*, vol. 102, no. 8, May 1991, p. 232).

The sanctifying of unholy places by Jesus is reflected again in the epistle to the Hebrews: 'Jesus also suffered outside the city gate in order to sanctify the people by his own blood. Let us then go to him outside the camp and bear the abuse he endured' (Hebrews 13:12–13).

18 The word used in Greek has a double sense: 'Martha served. The word is "deaconed" – and it is thought that the deacon was the only leadership role within the community which received this gospel' (Janet Morley, *Beforehand for the Burial: A Quiet Day for Holy Week, Monday April 1st 1985*, Women in Theology, p. 7). See also the note on *diakonia* in the chapter on Martha, note 7 on p. 81. The solemnity of the occasion is highlighted by the thrice repeated 'therefore' in the Greek: 'Therefore, six days before the Passover. . . . Therefore they gave a dinner for him. . . . Therefore Mary took a pound of costly perfume.' The effect of this is to indicate 'a sense of deliberate intention in the actions of Martha and Mary' (Morley, p. 7).

I could not eat much, and I slipped out halfway through the meal. No one suspected: they would have thought I was going to the kitchen. Instead I went to my room and knelt on the floor. I prayed with desperation. Then I undid my hair and let it fall freely.[19] I took out my precious vase, and carried it in front of me with slow solemnity into the dining room. I kept my eyes fixed rigidly on the vase: it was a luminous creamy white, with the lightest of grains, cool as marble, and almost as smooth. It had a beautiful shape, rising from a small foot to a full rounded body, with two curved handles, and tapering into a very narrow sealed neck. The jar alone must have accounted for a good part of the cost.

I hoped no one was watching, but Jesus must have seen me, for as I approached his chair he turned round to face me. He sat there, before me, his head at the level of my heart. His eyes were lifted with a look of expectation and humility, as though he knew what I was going to do. Around us the murmur of conversation continued.

I lifted the vase and <u>he bowed his head in readiness</u>. Suddenly I wondered how I was going to get the ointment out. How could I remove the seal? I panicked, for there was no time to lose. I took the neck between my two hands and snapped it off with a sudden, violent action.[20] The crack echoed through the room. Everyone instantly fell silent. There was no question of holding back any ointment now – everything was his. The creamy unguent poured out – over my hands, over Jesus' hair, down his face and over his clothes. The lavish smell hit me like a flash of fire.

I stood there stupidly and stared at what I had done, drenched in an overpowering fragrance that dulled my other senses. What

19 A good Jewess might pride herself in never letting anyone but her husband see her hair, and for a woman to unloose her hair was shameful in the eyes of the rabbis (see Joachim Jeremias, *Jerusalem in the Time of Jesus*, Fortress Press, Philadelphia, 1969, p. 360). Nonetheless, John 12:3 tells us that Mary wiped Jesus' feet with her hair, which must imply that she had loosened it.

20 Mark 14:3. 'It was common practice when anointing a dead body to break the bottle of ointment, and leave it with the corpse in the tomb' (Janet Morley, *Beforehand for the Burial*, p. 14).

I saw and heard and felt all came to me as though through a screen, while it was the smell – the *smell* – that was closer to me than my own breath. It cocooned me. It burned my lungs. I drowned in it.

I looked at what was in my left hand, and in my right. I saw jagged stone needles, poking through the smooth rich cream. I looked at the head that was by my heart. I saw richly oiled hair, through which the silvery sludge was still slipping. I wanted to run my hands through his locks, but I was still holding the jagged vase. I knelt down to put it on the floor, and Jesus caught me there, by the shoulders. His face said thank you, thank you. Oh no, I wanted to reply, it is for me to thank you, and the thought overpowered me so that I wept. The tears flowed down my cheeks as though to wash away all my fear and all my shame, all my sin and all my foolishness.

It was now not Jesus' hair but his feet that I grasped, slipping them out of his sandals. And then I remembered the story of how his own cousin, John the Baptist, had once said he was unworthy to kneel down and undo the strap of his sandals.[21] And that made me weep the more, for unthinkingly I had dared to do just that. I felt even more unworthy and sinful, and even more grateful that Jesus accepted me.[22] I kissed his feet with love and gratitude and begging, and my tears ran over them so fast that I pulled my hair round my face to wipe away the wetness. The pound of oily ointment was now dripping down all round us, so I gathered handfuls of the stuff and rubbed it into his feet. And so I kissed and washed and dried and massaged his feet, until they were the most beautiful feet that ever could be imagined, feet fit for the most precious and vulnerable of all actions, that of walking to the scaffold.[23]

21 This saying is quoted in Mark 1:7 and John 1:27.

22 Luke's overtones of the woman's sinfulness are captured here. We need not assume that she was a dramatic sinner, but that she had a strong sense of her sinfulness in the presence of Jesus.

23 The modern practice of aromatherapy for the dying operates on a similar principle. By making someone's body smell beautiful, one enables them to relax and feel serene and confident, at a time when they might otherwise feel their body is disgusting.

Having your feet washed is always pleasurable, even when done by a servant as a routine of hospitality,[24] but when it is done with the gratitude and intensity and tenderness of a lover it is a different experience altogether.[25] That is how I washed and dried and anointed Jesus' feet.[26] And I was aware of what a precious moment it was for us both.[27] Jesus' hands were still on my shoulders, affirming me, and after a while I looked up into his face and saw it full of softness and joy. Then the words came to me, from the royal psalm,

Therefore God, your God, has anointed you
with the oil of gladness beyond your companions;
your robes are all fragrant with myrrh.[28]

24 Such was the practice, when guests arrived footsore and dusty. To wash the feet with tepid water, and then anoint them with oil, is mentioned in the Talmud as a duty of maidservants.

25 The sexual overtones of Luke's version are captured here.

26 Even Elisabeth Moltmann-Wendel (whose critical remarks we looked at earlier: see note 1) appreciates the uniqueness of Mary's act of anointing: 'She came out of the shadows to become totally herself: the clumsy, loving, independent, tender, restrained and yet spontaneous woman' (*The Women Around Jesus*, p. 56). The anointing showed 'the revolutionary potential of love, which we keep wanting to reduce to the small and modest love of women, so that the calculating world remains undisturbed.' Mary is one of those women who have discovered 'that the gospel does not suppress their individuality but develops it, and amounts to the adventure of being themselves' (p. 58).

27 Elisabeth Moltmann-Wendel writes (with reference to the account in Mark's gospel): 'This Jesus needs people.... The betrayal by the disciples grieves him, and in Gethsemane this grief makes him tremble physically. The luxurious anointing comes from the comforting proximity of women: delight, enjoyment, pleasure, in a solitude that is becoming increasingly painful' (*The Women Around Jesus*, p. 102).

28 Psalm 45:7–8. These verses are also applied to Jesus by the writer of the epistle to the Hebrews (1:9). The psalm is dedicated, 'I address my verses to the king' (Psalm 45:1).

But while Jesus approved, no one else did. Out of the shocked silence I was now hearing horrified murmurs. I could catch one word, repeated here and there through the room. The word was 'waste'. Had I not said as much to myself, as I battled with myself outside the shop? Three hundred denarii. What a waste. But this was not the real waste. The real waste was the waste of Jesus' life – now so imminent. One waste was needed to commemorate the other. What I had broken was only a jar. What was about to be broken was much more precious – a body, Jesus' body.

One voice became clearer than the rest. I knew it at once. It came from one of Jesus' twelve, the one called Judas. I never trusted him. He had the audacity to say quite loudly to Jesus, 'That perfume must have been worth a prodigious sum. I would estimate it as around 300 denarii.' He was right, damn him. 'It should have been sold, and the money given to the poor.' Oh, the self-righteous tone of that complaint. I bet he never in his life gave a fraction of that sum to the poor. But the mood in the room supported him. I was mortified and confused – embarrassed for the sake of Martha and Lazarus – and I bit my lip and said nothing.[29]

But there was one person who was not against me. Jesus was imperious and angry and did not hesitate for a moment. 'Leave her alone. Leave her alone. What right have you to upset her?' The room fell silent again. Jesus looked around at the faces. They dropped their eyes to their plates. I dropped mine to his feet. Jesus was in total command – his mastery as total as that of the fragrance overpowering the house.

29 Like Jesus at his trial (Mark 14:61), Mary is silent in the face of her reproachers. She is 'like a sheep that before its shearers is silent' (Isaiah 53:7). According to Stephen Barton, Mark 'wants to cast the anonymous woman as a Christ-figure. Her extravagant love expressed in an act of self-giving which provokes conflict, is an anticipation in the narrative of what will happen to Jesus himself. . . . The story of Jesus himself follows the same pattern: acts of self-denying service; experiences of conflict which lead to his rejection and humiliation; and glorious vindication signified by the empty tomb' ('Mark as narrative: the story of the anointing woman, Mk 14:3–9', *The Expository Times*, vol. 102, no. 8, May 1991, pp. 232, 233).

Jesus challenged Judas: 'So you are so concerned about the poor, are you? You have plenty of chance to give to the poor. I'm delighted to hear you're so keen to get on with it.' He widened his gaze: 'Next week, next year, next decade, next century . . . you'll have as long as you want to give to the poor. You have the poor with you always,[30] but you will not always have me.' He did not stress the point, but I know what he meant: you will not ever have me again. It was as I knew – now or never.

And yet there was something of hope here in what Jesus was saying. Was he not telling me that I could go on loving and serving him after his death, in the person of the poor? What did he say again? 'You have the poor with you always, but you will not always have me.' And I remembered how he had taught us to feed the hungry and clothe the naked: 'Just as you did it to one of the least of my sisters or brothers, you did it to me.'[31] Jesus was saying something much more profound than claiming that he was one of the poor. He was claiming that he embodied the poor, he stood in not for one, but for all of them, and that any of them stood

∽

30 Jesus is quoting from the Old Testament, where the phrase is used to exhort people to attend to the poor. 'Since there will never cease to be some in need on the earth, I therefore command you, "Open your hand to the poor and needy neighbour in your land" ' (Deuteronomy 15:11). The point is exactly the opposite from the way it has sometimes been taken, to argue that there is no point in trying to create a society without poor people.

31 Matthew 25:40. In Matthew this teaching comes significantly immediately before the supper at Bethany. The songwriter Sydney Carter incorporates this insight into his hymn:

> Said Judas to Mary: 'Now what will you do
> With your ointment so rich and so rare?' . . . ,

in the verse,

> 'The poor of the world are my body', he said,
> 'To the end of the world they shall be.
> The bread and the blankets you give to the poor
> You'll find you have given to me', he said,
> 'You'll find you have given to me.'

in for him.[32] I had thought that I would lose him, but he was telling me I could find him a thousand times over, in the poor of the world. I could wash and kiss and anoint their feet for always, and I would be as close to him as I was now.[33]

And then I remembered also something else he taught us here at Bethany, which I believe he first announced at the very beginning of his ministry, in the synagogue at Nazareth: he applied to himself the words from the prophet Isaiah:

> The Spirit of the Lord is upon me,
> because he has anointed me
> to bring good news to the poor.[34]

If the anointing of Jesus was a commission to bring good news to the poor, then assuredly I was to follow the example of the one I had anointed. Clearly my life in future would take me beyond the cosy confines of Bethany – to the poor, wherever they were.

❧❧

32 Oscar, a poor fisherman from the basic ecclesial community at Solentiname, in Nicaragua, commented on this verse: 'If they'd sold it, it would have gone to only a small number of the poor, and the poor of the world are countless. On the other hand, when she offered it to Jesus, she was giving it, in his person, to all the poor' ('A Nicaraguan example: The alabaster bottle – Matthew 26:6–13' in *Voices from the Third World: Interpreting the Bible in the Third World*, ed. R. S. Sugirtharajah, SPCK, 1991, p. 412).

33 The liberation theologian from Brazil, Dominique Barbé, interprets Jesus' thought: 'When my body is no longer with you, when I shall no longer be visibly there, the poor will take my place and it will be they whom you must perfume, that is, help in every way and overwhelm them with the perfume of your love' (*Grace and Power*, Orbis, 1987, p. 20). Again, St Bernard comments on this text in one of his sermons on the Song of Songs, and points out that the reason Christ was anointed while living but not once he had died was to remind us to anoint (i.e. to care for) his living body, which is the Church (*Serm.* 12.6).

34 Jesus reads this passage from Isaiah 61:1 in the synagogue at Nazareth (Luke 4:18).

And Jesus continued, more quietly, 'It is a beautiful thing that she has done to me. It is a good deed.'[35] And I remembered how he had taught us that our 'good deeds' would shine like a lamp on a lampstand, to give glory to God.[36] And then he said, 'She has done what she could.' Oh, what comfort those words were. I did not want to be told: you have done great things; you have done marvels; you have done wonders. I would have known it was nonsense. But out of the oily mess and mish-mash of my attempt at love, these words were ointment to my soul: 'you have done what you could.' I could ask no more.[37]

And Jesus, always the teacher, explained to them quite simply what I had done. 'She has anointed my body beforehand for its burial.' That summed it up very well. Little did I know then that the anointing I performed on his living body would never be repeated after death. He had to be buried in a hurry before sundown, the next day was the sabbath, and when a group of women went early on the Sunday to anoint the body[38] it was already too late: he had gone.

And finally Jesus made the remark I told you of earlier. He said, 'I tell you solemnly, wherever the gospel is proclaimed in the

35 The Greek *kalon ergon* (Mark 14:6 and Matthew 26:10) means both a beautiful deed, and a good deed. According to Janet Morley, 'burying the dead was a traditional act of almsgiving, and Jesus is stating flatly: she *is* giving generously to the poor – I *am* one of the poor – what she has done for me is one of the good works' (*Beforehand for the Burial*, p. 15).
     From now on I follow Mark's account of Jesus' words.

36 *Kalon ergon* appears on only one other occasion in Matthew: 'No one after lighting a lamp puts it under the bushel basket, but on the lampstand, and it gives light to all in the house. In the same way, let your light shine before others, so that they may see your good works (*kala erga*) and give glory to your Father in heaven' (Matthew 5:15–16).

37 Alec McCowen writes: 'This is one of my favourite sayings of Jesus. It makes everyday life possible. It is a mini-guide to behaviour. It prevents nervous breakdowns' (*Personal Mark*, Collins Fount, 1984).

38 Luke 23:53–56 and Mark 16:1. Only in John is the body wrapped with myrrh and aloes.

whole world, what she has done will be told in remembrance of her.' That was such a big promise, so solemnly uttered, that the words seemed to echo around the room as we took them in, all of us incredulous, I highly honoured, some of the others resentful and rejecting.

That was the last time I saw Jesus. But I heard later of another solemn supper a few days later, on the very eve of his death.[39] I heard that what happened between us that night in Bethany was recalled there, in an upper room in Jerusalem. Jesus must have found it so moving to have his feet washed, that he wanted to hand on the experience to those he loved.[40] And so, like me, he went

39 I do not recount the events of the Last Supper anywhere in this book. But it would be a mistake to deduce from that omission that I accept the widely promulgated but highly questionable claim that women were excluded from the Last Supper.

On the contrary, the balance of probability tips in favour of them being there, following the Ricci principle (see note 40 on p. 136 below), that is, that 'every time the writings are silent about women and do not mention their presence it will be quite unfounded to deduce their absence' (Maria di Magdala e le Molte Altre, pp. 20–1). What we do know is that the twelve were present at the Last Supper (Matthew 26:20 and Mark 14:17); what we do not know is who else from the wider group of 'disciples' was there as well (Matthew 26:17 and Mark 14:12). The group of women travelling companions, including Mary Magdalene (see note 24 on p. 124), were more likely to have been present than absent. And we can say with confidence, on the basis of Ricci's analysis, that whether or not the women were there they would in any case not have been mentioned.

However, it is a mistake in my view to make too much hang on the question of whether or not women were there. (Many people nowadays argue that women could only be admitted to the priesthood if they were present at the Last Supper – a line of reasoning which contains several blatantly invalid leaps of logic.) By omitting the Last Supper from this book I hope to avoid the implication that the question of women's presence or absence there is significant, and I also wish to highlight the theological importance of the Supper at Bethany, which has suffered so much from being overshadowed by the Jerusalem Supper.

40 In washing their feet he showed he loved them 'to the end' (John 13:1).

on his knees before them and washed and dried their feet.[41] And he told them in their turn to do the same to others. It was an action that spoke of love, of service, and of forgiveness – forgiveness given, and forgiveness received with thanksgiving. It was a purifying and intimate experience – in Jerusalem, as at Bethany.

And, as I did at Bethany, he made a gift, breaking and pouring out, as a sign of overwhelming love. For me it was an alabaster jar broken, and a perfume poured out. For him it was bread broken, and wine poured out – simple gifts, but steeped in meaning for him, for he said it was his body broken, and his blood poured out.[42] And again he made a solemn pronouncement about the memory of that moment – 'Do this in remembrance of me' – just as he had promised that my action would be remembered – 'What she has done will be told in remembrance of her'.[43]

41 John 13:1–17. Note that in John the Last Supper does not fall on the Passover (which was to be six days after the supper at Bethany, according to John), but beforehand.

42 The two suppers follow directly on from each other in Mark, as in Matthew. 'These two stories correspond and contrast. In each, there is a ritual action which is interpreted as symbolizing Jesus's death. In each, there is a reference to Jesus's body (Mark 14:8, 22). And both episodes end with a saying of Jesus beginning with the pronouncement formula: "Truly, I say to you" (14:9, 25). Such correspondences reinforce the idea that the anointing woman is a Christ-figure' (Stephen Barton, 'Mark as narrative: the story of the anointing woman, Mk 14:3–9', *The Expository Times*, vol. 102, no. 8, May 1991, p. 232).

43 1 Corinthians 11:24, 25 and Luke 22:19. Professor Christopher Rowland comments: 'It is quite extraordinary to note that the words "what she has done will be told in memory of her" (14:9) are similar to the words used by Jesus according to 1 Corinthians 11:23 when he speaks of the repeated act of sharing bread and wine ("Do this in remembrance of me"). In other words the woman's place in Christian memory and story is guaranteed. Not only did she act in a priestly way by anointing the messiah who was to suffer and die but also her action was placed on a par with the memorial of the death for which she was preparing. The most priestly moment in the gospel story, the anointing of the messiah, is performed by a woman' (Christopher Rowland, 'How the poor can liberate the Bible', *Priests and People*, October 1992, p. 371).

The other result of my action was horrific. That same Judas was so disapproving of what I had done and of how Jesus had defended me that he went to the chief priests and betrayed him to them. I had paid 300 denarii for Jesus' oil; he was paid 30 pieces of silver for Jesus' blood.[44]

And so I had done even more than I realized. Not only did I show public recognition of the fact that Jesus was going to die, but I actually performed the act that set that death in motion. I suppose you could say I killed him. If he was the sacrifice, I was the priest.

44 The chief priests call it 'blood money' in Matthew 27:6. The story of Judas' betrayal is found in Matthew 26:14–16, Mark 14:10–11 and Luke 22:3–6.

THE STORY OF
M A R Y

OF MAGDALA
WHO TURNED, AND TURNED AGAIN, TO FIND
NEW LIFE

My name is Mary Magdalene. You have probably heard my name
mentioned as one of Jesus' women disciples. There were quite a few
of us over the years, but I was one of the earliest and most constant
companions. Perhaps that is why my name tends to be put at the
top of the list.[1] Or perhaps it is because Jesus and I were very
close. Or perhaps it is because of what happened at the end – when
he made me the first witness of his resurrection. But let me not spoil
the story.

I was known as Mary Magdalene, because there were several
of us who were called Mary among Jesus' followers. There was
Mary the mother of James and Joses, and the wife of Clopas, who

1 Matthew, Mark and Luke all put Mary Magdalene's name first when
   naming the group of women disciples (Luke 8:1–3; 24:10; Matthew
   27:55–56; Mark 15:40–41). John also makes her one of the four
   meriting special mention, though he puts her name last (John 19:25).
   However, John puts her together with Jesus' blood relatives, Mary of
   Nazareth and her sister: 'The fact that she is named together with
   those who are strictly relatives is a different way of establishing her
   importance from that of the synoptics' (Carla Ricci, *Maria di Magdala
   e le Molte Altre*, M. d'Auria Editore, Naples, 1991, p. 149).
       Lilia Sebastiani claims unambiguously: 'Mary of Magdala is the
   most important woman and the one with the greatest presence in
   the gospels and indeed in the entire New Testament. This is an idea
   which can sound most surprising, even jarring, for those who are used
   to seeing the mother of Jesus in this role. . . . Mary of Magdala is
   named explicitly twelve times in the gospels, and more than that if
   we take into account the two implicit mentions ("the women who had
   come with him from Galilee" in Luke's gospel)' (*Tra/Sfigurazione*,
   p. 39). However, Sebastiani has chosen to pay scant attention to the
   early chapters of Luke, where Mary of Nazareth plays a very important role, but where the historical status of the stories is highly
   questionable.

often went around with me: sometimes people would call us 'Mary Magdalene and the other Mary'.[2] And then of course there was Jesus' mother Mary, the wife of Joseph of Nazareth.[3] And there was another Mary, with a sister called Martha and a brother called Lazarus, who lived in Bethany: she did not follow Jesus on the road as some of us did, but she was very close to him. Normally, as you know, women take their second name from their closest male relative.[4] Because I was not married, and had no children,

2 Matthew 27:61; 28:1. We may hypothesize that 'Mary [the wife] of Clopas', who John tells us was at the cross (19:25), may have been the same Mary as the mother of James and Joses, who Matthew (27:56) and Mark (15:40) tell us was at the cross, and whom Matthew also apparently refers to as 'the other Mary' (27:61 and 28:1). If the women are different, then there are even more Marys.

To this Lilia Sebastiani adds two more Marys from the early Church – the mother of John Mark (Acts 12:12) and one of Paul's collaborators (Romans 16:6) – making six (or seven) Marys in total in the New Testament (Tra/Sfigurazione, p.12).

3 The prevalence of the name 'Mary' among Jesus' followers is alluded to in the Gospel of Philip (see also note 23 on p. 123 below): 'There were three who walked with the Lord at all times, Mary his mother and her sister and Magdalene, whom they called his consort (koinōnos). For Mary was his sister and his mother and his consort' (The Gospel of Philip, 107: trans. and comm. Robert McL. Wilson, Mowbray, 1962, p. 35).

4 Women in the gospels are identified by their husband or son, even to the extent of the lengthy and clumsy phrase 'the mother of the sons of Zebedee' (Matthew 27:56). Today women are still named after their nearest male relative, for their surname comes either from their husband or their father.

Lilia Sebastiani points out that because Mary Magdalene is the exception to this rule, 'one of the basic elements in the enigma of the Magdalene consists precisely in the fact that she does not belong to any man: she cannot be placed in relationship with any man except with Jesus. From this, endless intuitions and speculations have arisen. . . . The myth of the sinner has rested, among other factors, upon this absence of reassuring family ties' (Tra/Sfigurazione, p. 41).

According to Carla Ricci, Jesus undermines this way of identifying

I could not be named after either husband or son, so I was named after the town I came from – Mary of Magdala,[5] or Mary Magdalene.

Magdala is on the Sea of Galilee, just south of Capernaum, where Jesus spent a lot of his time,[6] because he had a house there for a while.[7] Peter's in-laws also lived there.[8] But Jesus spent a lot of time in all those towns around the lake, like Gennesaret[9] and

women by their family roles in the episode of the 'true relatives', when Jesus says, 'My mother and my siblings are those who hear the word of God and do it' (Luke 8:21). She says Jesus' relationship with women 'was not founded on an acceptance of fixed "roles" that over-shadow the person – "daughter of", "wife of", "mother of", "connected to" – but rather on their fidelity to the word of God, as they hear it and put it into practice' (*Maria di Magdala e le Molte Altre*, p. 103).

5 Magdala was a city in Galilee, on the plain of Gennesaret, on the western bank of the Sea of Galilee, about five kilometres north of Tiberias. It is identified with Mejdel, an Arab village which existed on that site up until 1948, when it was swept away in the Arab–Israeli war. It was also known at the time of Jesus as Tarichea (from the Greek *tarikhos*, salt fish) and the Jewish historian Josephus said that Tarichea had 40,000 inhabitants, with many artisans other than fisherfolk, and with a fleet of 230 boats. Rabbinical literature from the first century on gave the city an ill repute, linking its corruption to its wealth.

6 Capernaum is mentioned sixteen times in the gospels.

7 This is implied by Mark 2:1 – 'when he returned to Capernaum after some days, it was reported that he was at home' – and by Matthew's parallel – 'he crossed the sea and came to his own town' (Matthew 9:1). Another suggestion of it is found in Mark 9:33 – 'Then they came to Capernaum; and when he was in the house he asked them. . . .'

8 Mark 1:21–29, Luke 4:31–38. John tells us that Peter and Andrew came from Bethsaida, which is only a mile or two east of Capernaum.

9 Many sick were brought to him here (Matthew 14:34, Mark 6:53).

Tiberias,[10] Bethsaida[11] and Chorazin.[12] And Cana[13] was not far off either – about ten miles west of the lakeside. Then of course his home town of Nazareth was only another couple of miles beyond Cana, but he steered clear of there after one disastrous day when they tried to stone him: it was hard for those who had watched him grow up to realize he was someone quite out of the ordinary.[14] And so he did the rounds, preaching in the synagogues, healing in the market squares, accepting hospitality from those ready to receive him, and moving on to the next town.

My parents worked in the fishing industry, which was what nearly everyone in Magdala did, and they made quite a lot of money from it.[15] I grew up without any material deprivations,

10 Not mentioned in the gospels by name, but implied by Jesus' words at Capernaum in Mark 1:38–39: ' "Let us go on to the neighbouring towns, so that I may proclaim the message there also; for that is what I came out to do." And he went throughout Galilee, proclaiming the message in their synagogues. . . .' Visits to Magdala are even more implied by these words, since Magdala stood halfway between Capernaum and Tiberias.

11 At Bethsaida Jesus heals the blind man who saw people as trees walking (Mark 8:22ff.). Jesus sends the disciples to Bethsaida after the feeding of the 5,000 in Mark (6:45), while in Luke (9:10) Jesus and the disciples have already gone to Bethsaida when the crowd follow him, leading up to the miraculous feeding. According to John, Philip came from Bethsaida (John 1:44 and 12:21), as also did Andrew and Peter.

12 Jesus said that mighty works were done here, as also in Bethsaida and Capernaum (Matthew 11:21–23, Luke 10:12–15).

13 As well as attending the famous marriage at Cana (John 2:1–11), Jesus goes to Cana in John 4:46.

14 Luke 4:16–30. But although Luke uses this story for the opening of Jesus' ministry in Galilee, it is clear even from the Lukan text that he had previously ministered in Capernaum (Luke 4:23).

15 Lilia Sebastiani suggests: 'It is possible, even if not certain, that she came from a family that was very comfortably off; and if the Magdalene did come from a rich or renowned family, or perhaps

and yet I do not mind telling you that before I met Jesus I was a mess.[16] A lot of people might say that of themselves before they met Jesus, but I really was. I was sick mentally and emotionally, intellectually and spiritually, socially and morally, and even phy-

∞

one with Greek influence, that could make more plausible the fact that she seems to enjoy a freedom of movement and of auto-determination unusual for an ordinary Hebrew woman in the time of Jesus' (*Tra/Sfigurazione*, p. 42). See also note 5 on p. 117 above.

16 I have portrayed this mess as manic depression (see also note 22 on p. 122) rather than the traditional prostitution. The tradition that Mary Magdalene was a prostitute is among the most extraordinary and implausible inventions ever woven out of gospel texts. The reasoning behind the tradition followed this far-fetched course: the woman who anointed Jesus in Luke (7:36–50) was 'a sinner'; the scandal of Jesus allowing himself to be touched by a sinner (Luke 7:39) may imply that she was a prostitute (this despite the fact that Luke uses a different word for prostitute elsewhere: 15:30); the woman who anoints Jesus in John's gospel is Mary of Bethany (John 12:1–8); therefore Mary of Bethany was a prostitute; Luke's anointing story is immediately followed by the information that Mary Magdalene was one of Jesus' followers, and that seven devils had been driven out of her; therefore Mary Magdalene was a terrible sinner (this despite the fact that this exorcism is given as an example of healing from infirmity, 8:2, and that exorcism usually refers to illness rather than sin); therefore Mary Magdalene may have been the sinner referred to a moment before (this despite the fact that no link is made with the previous mention, but remember that it has been decided that the 'sinner' was called Mary); therefore Mary Magdalene was a prostitute. Strangely the idea has remained that Mary Magdalene was a prostitute even after her supposed identification with Mary of Bethany – on which it depends – has been largely forgotten.

The first step towards this conflation of three separate women was made by Jerome, when he linked the seven demons with the previous story of sin and love: *Maria Magdalena ipsa est, a qua septem daemonia expulerat; ut ubi abundaverat peccatum, superabundaret gratia* ('Mary Magdalene was that woman from whom he had driven out seven demons, in order that where sin had been abundant, grace might be more abundant', *Hier. ep.* 59, 4: *Corpus Scriptorum Ecclesiasticorum Latinorum*, 54, 545).

sically as well.[17] Sometimes I sat at home, moping and moaning, making everyone's life a misery, shaking and trembling with insecurity, twisting my hair between my fingers until I pulled it out and left my scalp red and raw. At other times I was quite the opposite – so energetic and determined that people could not stop me talking, could not stop me running up bills which my parents then had to pay, could not stop me promising the impossible, could not hold me back from running through the streets on some mad scheme or other. Then the world seemed to me peopled with idiots, and I did not hesitate to tell them so. If they would not listen I would scream at them. When I became very ill, from time to time, I would hallucinate.

I first met Jesus when he came to our synagogue in

The tradition of Mary Magdalene as prostitute has become almost immovable in our received tradition, largely because of the rich artistic work it has inspired. Mary Magdalene is portrayed as an emotional, even hysterical woman with long, loose red hair and a brilliant scarlet dress, weeping at the cross or seeing the risen Jesus in the garden. Though this character has its own appeal, the drawback is that it has also reinforced the identification of women with sexual temptation, for the two classic ways in which a woman can follow Jesus are summed up in the archetypes of Mary the blue-robed mother of Jesus, who has never known sex, and the red-robed Mary Magdalene who has repented of knowing sex.

It is also to be deplored that the prostitute tradition has robbed Mary Magdalene of her dignified stance as leading woman disciple and first witness to the resurrection: from being an example of women's leadership and ministry she has been sidetracked into being an example of women's weakness, changeability and need for repentance. Elisabeth Moltmann-Wendel comments: 'Anyone who loves the biblical Mary Magdalene, and compares her with the "Christian" Mary Magdalene, must get very angry. . . . The great sinner, of whom Luke speaks (Luke 7), and Mary Magdalene, whom all four gospels report, have as little to do with each other as Peter and Judas' (*The Women Around Jesus*, p. 64).

17 Mary was possessed by seven demons (Luke 8:2, Mark 16:9), so it seems an appropriate literary device to describe her problems in a sevenfold way. See also notes 21 and 22 on p. 122.

Magdala.[18] He stood up and spoke about the way God wanted the world to be – a world where the sick are made well and victims become free[19] – and I thought, 'Yes, that's for me. I am sick. I am a victim. I want to be better. Let me out of this prison of my mind.' The way he spoke was as marvellous as the things he said. You felt you could put your whole self in his hands and trust him utterly. At the end of the service he was surrounded by people, clamouring to hear him or ask a question, and I lacked the confidence to push my way in, so I sadly headed for home. Then I heard my name called, 'Mary!', and it was as though the voice was coming from my own heart, it felt so close to me. I turned, and there was Jesus. He had stepped out of the knot of people to call me back. I felt my whole life had changed in that simple decision to turn round when he called me. I was chosen. I was named. I was selected. I was wanted. And I, who had always been so resistant to those who tried to help me, would never turn down that offer or turn away from that voice. God knows how he knew my name or how he knew I needed him so badly. I moved towards him and answered him with a single word, the word for a religious leader. 'Rabbi!' I said. I was telling him, 'You will be my leader. I will follow you.'[20]

18 This was Jesus' usual way into a new town: Matthew 4:23, Mark 1:39, Luke 4:44. It may be that women would have been segregated in a gallery: from a survey of the evidence Ben Witherington concludes, 'It is not certain when the practice of having special galleries for women in the synagogues began, though apparently they existed in Trajan's time' (*Women in the Ministry of Jesus*, p. 7).

19 See the specimen sermon Luke gives from Nazareth (Luke 4:17–27).

20 This imaginary meeting reflects the post-resurrection encounter of Jesus with Mary Magdalene (John 20:11–18). In Mary's case, where so little is recorded about someone who is nonetheless admitted to be constantly in Jesus' company and the chief of the women followers, so that quite a lot of imaginative reconstruction is called for, we find particularly relevant the words of Carla Ricci on the need for what she calls an 'exegesis of silence'. 'One wishes to go back, and retrace the path, and dig deep in the texts that have

When you have very deep and serious problems, it takes a while to become a new person. Jesus worked hard and long with me, and there were a number of turning points[21] before I could honestly say I was free of what used to possess me.[22] Jesus spent time with me. He cared about what happened to me. He committed himself never to give up on me. When you understand that you will

come down to us to find the *traces* of a significant presence of women and to discover *indicative and revealing fragments* of a much fuller reality which lies hidden. Like a subterranean river, from time to time it trickles up into the texts, emerges above ground and so reveals its permanent presence' (*Maria di Magdala e le Molte Altre*, p. 23). One of the silences concerns the call of the women who followed Jesus: 'If it is not recorded in the texts that the women are called in the way we are told some of the men are, it is still clear that they too are welcomed and chosen by him, even apart from the likelihood that their call has not been handed down within that vast silence that embraces them' (*Maria di Magdala e le Molte Altre*, p. 192).

21 Luke tells us that Jesus had cast out seven demons from Mary Magdalene (Luke 8:2) and so does Mark, in the longer ending to the gospel (Mark 16:9). Seven was a favourite, symbolic number, occurring 88 times in the New Testament (Ricci, *Maria di Magdala e le Molte Altre*, pp. 141–2), e.g. 'If the same person sins against you seven times a day, and turns back to you seven times and says, "I repent", you must forgive' (Luke 17:4). Mary's seven demons probably simply implied that she had a very severe case of illness, rather than that there were seven stages on the route to recovery. See also note 17 on p. 120.

22 Illnesses that came from within, and therefore had no clear natural cause like a wound, were often spoken of as the work of demons: '. . . it is not the redactor's intention to indicate the physical or psychological causes of the suffering at a purely human level, but rather to present it under a particular light: a violence brought about by a power of evil. . . . According to the understanding of the age, this woman was considered victim of an illness that was not clearly explicable, and that involved a thoroughly complicated psychophysical state (evidenced by the use of the number seven), all of which made her belong to the category of those possessed by

understand why we became so close.[23] We had been through a lot together. You could say Jesus went through the wilderness with me. It is not something you ever forget.

By the time I was fully well it seemed a foregone conclusion that I would stay with Jesus. But it is not something I ought ever to take for granted, for we were a very fortunate group who were

demons. The only clue we have for reconstructing the nature of the disturbances from which Mary of Magdala suffered is the expression that we are examining. In the light of the knowledge we have today in the medical and psychological fields we can formulate hypotheses. It could perhaps be a matter of disturbances in her psychic character. Perhaps she was a woman of great sensitivity, whose equilibrium had not coped with the impact of life's very grievous problems, which were even more evident for a woman living in Palestine at the time of Jesus. A sensitivity that perhaps she had not had space to express herself and to organize herself; a repressed psychic energy that had not found creative and constructive forms of expression; a tension, a vital force that had been repressed and perhaps had ended up unbalancing the mind of this woman. . . . Mary of Magdala, therefore, no matter what hypotheses or objective factors there may be relating to her condition, is a woman "dispossessed of herself" ' (Ricci, *Maria di Magdala e le Molte Altre*, pp. 145–7).

23 According to two gospels, the *Gospel of Philip* and the *Gospel of Mary*, which were not accepted as reliable and were not incorporated into the accepted scriptures, Jesus loved Mary Magdalene more than any other disciple, male or female, and gave her privileged knowledge not available to the twelve. However, these documents, which form part of the collection found at Nag Hammadi in Upper Egypt, are not likely to throw historical light on the life of Jesus. They come from heretical, gnostic circles (in fact from followers of Valentinus) and their aim is to provide theological justification for a group of 'mature' Christians, initiated into secret mysteries (such as that the creator of the world is not God), to free themselves from the ordinary Church authorities. Mary of Magdala therefore acts as a role model for the heretics.

The *Gospel of Philip* says: 'The consort of [Christ is] Mary Magdalene. [The Lord loved Mary] more than [all] the disciples, and kissed her on her [mouth] often. . . They said to him, "Why do you

invited to go with him from town to town.[24] While others clamoured for the privilege of an odd word, we were his constant companions, soaking up his beliefs and attitudes, sharing in his moods, and – increasingly as time went on – making our own contributions to his work.

love her more than all of us?" The Saviour answered and said to them, "Why do I not love you like her?" ' (*The Gospel of Philip*, 111; trans. and comm. Robert McL. Wilson, p. 39).

The *Gospel of Mary* contains a longer passage on Mary Magdalene, in the context of the disciples' grieving and despair after the departure of the risen Christ: 'Mary stood up, greeted them all, and said to her brethren, "Do not weep and do not grieve nor be irresolute, for his grace will be entirely with you". . . She turned their hearts to the Good, and they began to discuss the words of the [Saviour]. Peter said to Mary, "Sister, we know that the Saviour loved you more than the rest of women. Tell us the words of the Saviour which you remember – which you know (but) we do not nor have we heard them." '

Mary recounts a vision, at the end of which Peter says: ' "Did he really speak privately with a woman (and) not openly to us? Are we to turn about and all listen to her? Did he prefer her to us?' Then Mary wept and said to Peter, "My brother Peter, what do you think? Do you think that I thought this up myself in my heart, or that I am lying about the Saviour?" Levi answered and said to Peter, "Peter, you have always been hot-tempered. Now I see you contending against the woman like the adversaries. But if the Saviour made her worthy, who are you indeed to reject her? Surely the Saviour knows her very well. That is why he loved her more than us" ' (*The Gospel of Mary*, in *The Nag Hammadi Library in English*, ed. James M. Robinson et al., Harper and Row, New York, 1977, pp. 472–3).

24 We know about women being in Jesus' regular travelling party from Luke 8:1–3: '. . . he went on through cities and villages, proclaiming and bringing the good news of the kingdom of God. The twelve were with him, as well as some women who had been cured of evil spirits and infirmities: Mary, called Magdalene . . . and many others, who provided for them out of their resources.' This is confirmed (if only by way of a retrospective comment) by Matthew 27:55–56: 'Many women were also there, looking on from a disance; they had followed Jesus from Galilee and had provided for

I put in the pool of finance my own allowance from my family. It was not vast but I found it went further when there were a dozen or more of us living frugally with minimum expenses than it did when I was wasting money on extravagances for myself alone. Later on we had some richer followers who put in more money, like Joanna (the wife of Herod's steward, Chuza), who left her husband behind and became one of our travelling party;[25] and there

him. Among them were Mary Magdalene. . . .' (Mark 15:40–41 is a parallel).

Ben Witherington comments: 'There is little reason to question the authenticity of the information that women travelled with and served Jesus and the disciples as this was conduct which was unheard of and considered scandalous in Jewish circles' (*Women in the Ministry of Jesus*, p. 117).

When we consider stories like the Gerasene demoniac, which tells of a man begging to follow Jesus but being sent back home instead (Luke 8:38) we realize, says Ricci, that 'it is Jesus alone who decides who are the people who should take part in his following' (*Maria di Magdala e le Molte Altre*, p. 192). It is therefore 'certain beyond question that Jesus wanted a group of women among the restricted and privileged circle that lived with him, going from village to village' (p. 60). 'In a vision of the people who are placed around the Master as in concentric circles, the women are placed by Luke on the first level together with the twelve as regards the journeying and their proximity to Jesus. The women are witnesses to his life and preaching and particularly to that privileged preaching which is reserved for the narrowest group of followers' (p. 171).

Lilia Sebastiani, too, makes the point that 'we are not told of any man who, having been healed by Jesus, was made his disciple. For Mary of Magdala and for the other women the healing has become an integral salvation, a change of life, therefore a "conversion"' (*Tra/Sfigurazione*, pp. 24–5).

25 Elisabeth Moltmann-Wendel has a most interesting chapter on Joanna in *The Women Around Jesus*. Ben Witherington also comments: 'What husband (Jew or Gentile) would willingly have let his wife leave home and family to become a follower of an itinerant Jewish preacher? Yet Luke 8:3 probably indicates that Joanna, the wife of Chuza, had done this' (*Women in the Ministry of Jesus*, p. 126). The explanation for

was another woman called Susanna; then there were Joseph of Arimathea and Nicodemus, who never journeyed with us but let us know they would underwrite any expenses.[26]

When a group moves around like that there are a whole host of practical considerations – where you are going to get your clothes washed and how you are going to get your sandals repaired, where you are going to pay your taxes[27] and what you are going to eat that day. Inevitably we women tended to be better at organizing these practical details of life: it seems to be like that the world over. But that was far from all we did.[28] Our most

this scandalous behaviour is found in Jesus' teaching on the new family of God taking precedence over blood relationships: see note 36 on p. 41, note 51 on p. 49, note 4 on p. 116 and note 31 on p. 128.

   Joanna is mentioned in Luke 8:3 and 24:10, and Susanna just in Luke 8:3.

26 It was Joseph of Arimathea, a rich man (Matthew 27:57ff.) and a respected councillor (Mark 15:43ff.) who provided an expensive rock-hewn tomb for Jesus, and Nicodemus, a Pharisee and a Jewish leader (John 3:1ff. and 7:50) who brought an extravagant quantity of myrrh and aloes to bind up with the body (John 19:39).

27 Financial matters are one area where traditionally the man is in charge, but Luke's information that the women provided for the group 'out of their resources' suggests that much of the economic management in this party was done by women.

28 Luke 8:1–3 tells us that the women 'ministered' to Jesus (some texts say to the group) out of their resources. Matthew 27:55–56 also tells us that they 'ministered' to him. The Greek verb is *diakonein*, about which there has been much interesting discussion recently (see note 7 on p. 81). Its spread of meanings stretches from serving at table ('For who is greater, the one who is at the table or the one who serves? Is it not the one at the table? But I am among you as one who serves': Luke 22:27) to serving as deacons ('Let them first be tested; then, if they prove themselves blameless, let them serve as deacons': 1 Timothy 3:10). The associated noun, *diakonos*, is a term Paul regularly uses to describe his ministry (2 Corinthians 3:6, Ephesians

important task really was to listen and learn,[29] for we were being prepared for the coming work of spreading the good news of Jesus.[30] He did not ask us to follow him out of courtesy or compassion but because he needed to educate and strengthen a carefully selected group for the future Church.

As time went on we began to share in Jesus' ministry, and this happened through a natural progression. You see, while the crowds of sick people were gathering to see Jesus, there was an obvious need for us to welcome them and ask what help they were looking for. We would try to ensure that they queued in a fair way, while also of course giving priority to urgent cases. As we organized the sick and troubled we found we were beginning in our own way to minister to them, by being compassionate and reassuring and

3:7, Colossians 1:23, 25). The verb will not of itself bear the weight either of the interpretation that the women's work was one of preparing meals, or of the interpretation that they were working in a capacity similar to St Paul.

29 We remember how Jesus commends Mary of Bethany for having 'chosen the better part' in giving priority to listening to his teaching over attending to the practical details of a meal. Undoubtedly Jesus would have applied the same criteria to his women companions, and expected them to share in the teaching he wanted to impart to his inner group. We have evidence that the women were in the group who received the prophecy of his passion, from the message of the angels 'Remember how he told you, while he was still in Galilee . . .' (Luke 24:6) and from the assertion that the women 'remembered his words' (Luke 24:8).

   Even the forthrightly sexist first letter of Paul to Timothy allows women to listen and learn, though not to spread the gospel: 'Let a woman learn in silence with full submission. I permit no woman to teach or to have authority over a man; she is to keep silent' (1 Timothy 2:11–12).

30 Despite texts like 1 Timothy, we do have evidence that women were involved in spreading the gospel. We know this not only from the involvement of women in ministry in the early Church, for example Phoebe the deacon, Priscilla (also called Prisca), and the other women of Romans 16, but also from the fact that Jesus makes Mary of Magdala the apostle to the apostles in bringing news of the resurrection (see note 64 on p. 148).

responding to their needs in so far as we were able. Many people preferred to speak to one of Jesus' male disciples, but some, especially children and their mothers, found it easier to approach a woman.

Gradually, according to what came naturally to each of us, we found we were beginning to prepare people for their meeting with Jesus – speaking about the love and mercy of God, praying with them, and so on. And then, as we prayed with them, we began to find that some of us had the gift of healing too. Some of us had the gift of communicating peace and trust. And some of us had the gift of explaining Jesus' teaching in a clear way. When the men talked about their ministry, they made it sound as though it was they who had done everything, but as can be seen the world over, women always do a great deal which is unacknowledged. It was not so much that Jesus gave us new responsibilities, but that they grew naturally out of the situation, because of the pressures of attending to the needs of the people.[31] And so it came about that I, who had been the sickest of any of Jesus' followers, developed into one of his most active co-workers.

As I have said, I was with Jesus from the time of his early ministry in the towns round the Sea of Galilee. They were good

31 Ben Witherington says: 'There can be little doubt that the family was almost the exclusive sphere of influence for Jewish women in the first century AD' (*Women in the Ministry of Jesus*, p. 2). And so: 'For a Jewish woman to leave home and travel with a rabbi was not only unheard of, it was scandalous' (p. 117). It was even more scandalous, he says, when the travelling companions were not considered respectable women. H. Daniel-Rops gives a picture of women in that society excluded from social and public life, and shut up at home where 'often the windows that overlooked the streets were closed with a grating so that they should not be seen' (*La vie quotidienne en Palestine au temps de Jésus*, Hachette, Paris, 1961, p. 157).

Given this fact, and given the way Jesus releases women from family stereotypes (Matthew 12:47ff., Mark 3:32ff., Luke 8:20ff., Matthew 10:35ff., Luke 12:52ff.) and from traditional role models (as in the Martha and Mary story, Luke 10:38ff.), Carla Ricci judges that it is 'absolutely inconceivable that the women in his group were shut into traditional roles' (*Maria di Magdala e le Molte Altre*, p. 190).

times, when we were still thrilled to turn up in a new place and see a crowd of people flock together, when his preaching was free of the conflict that overhung the later period. It was exciting – more than that, exhilarating – and we felt we were transforming the world, village by village. Those were the days when everyone wanted to follow Jesus. Many began to come along after him, but few lasted. Many were called, but few were chosen.

One of the early turning points came when Jesus said we would cross the sea to go to the country of the Gadarenes. The crowd was beginning to reach such a size that Jesus was quite worn out and we needed to escape for a while. It was a situation which was to recur many times later but it was only just beginning to be a problem at that date. But one of our group was reluctant to get into the boat and set off, because he did not know when we would be back. His father was close to death, he pointed out, so he needed to stay within easy access; he would like to remain behind until after the funeral and rejoin the party later. Jesus was not very sympathetic, because you could not be in the inner group of journeying companions and still expect to be free to pop off home on other commitments. Those who were followers had to give up everything, and if you were not in a position to do that you could not expect to be one of his travelling party. We could not arrange a future rendezvous, because we did not know where we would be at any time ahead: we had to respond to the situation as we met it along the road. So that was the end of that follower. He could have chosen a different way of supporting Jesus, while staying within his own town, but he did not – he just fell away. Many others dropped out in similar fashion at later dates.

So the rest of us climbed into the boat, knowing that by that shaky, rocking step we were also stepping out in commitment to an unknown future, and we set off for the south-east corner of the lake. Going there would get rid of the crowds, because it was the furthest point from the towns where we had worked. We were really tested on that journey. A storm blew up and it was so bad that we honestly thought we would drown. The waves were pounding into the boat, so that it was filling up with water faster than we could bail it out. We were frozen from the wetness of the spray and the fierceness of the wind, and we were only kept warm by the panic-stricken pounding of our hearts. Going through my head was the thought that to follow Jesus I had had to put my very life at risk, and the terrified anxiety that this was the moment that it was demanded of me.

He meanwhile was asleep – absolutely exhausted from his work of attending to so many sick people – though how he could have slept through such a storm we could none of us understand. Eventually we shook him awake, screaming that we were going to die. He got up and addressed the waves and the wind, saying, 'Peace. Be still.' The storm did indeed die down, and there was a great peace inside me when I saw we were saved: it was as though he had commanded our hearts as well as the storm. Then he gave us a little ticking off for having insufficient faith, and went straight back to sleep.

When we landed we were in a desolate area around Gadara, and we knew we were out of Jewish territory because there was a simply enormous herd of pigs feeding on the hills. (Pigs are unclean for Jews.) At least here we should be free of the crowds. Then suddenly we saw a madman racing down to meet us.[32] This really was going to be a difficult journey – as though Jesus were leading us through all the trials of the underworld. The madman was naked and dirty and violent. He had bits of broken chains around his legs and arms, where he had fought himself free of restraint. He kept on picking up stones and attacking his own body with them, and we were all terrified he was going to throw them at us as well. We huddled nervously behind Jesus, ready to duck or run or seek cover. But Jesus walked on towards him.

The madman began shouting out fiercely at the top of his voice, 'What have you to do with me, Jesus, son of the most high God?! Do not torment me!' and then he fell on his knees and foamed and shouted and lurched. Jesus took him by the shoulders, and he flailed around still more violently. We could hear Jesus asking, 'What is your name?' and the madman (or the demons inside

32 Matthew 8:21–34, Mark 4:35 – 5:20, Luke 8:22–39. I have followed Matthew's order in putting the three incidents in succession – the disciple who wanted to bury his father, the storm at sea and the Gadarene swine; Mark and Luke have the second and third incidents but without the first (though it appears elsewhere in Luke 9:59ff.). But I have taken some details of the Gadarene swine story from Mark and Luke, including the fact of there being one madman rather than two. I have not attempted to 'explain' the miracle, and really see little point in doing so. Extraordinary events are recounted, and we can leave it at that.

him) replying, 'Legion! There is a whole legion of us!' I must admit I was afraid of what would happen to Jesus, for the power and fury of that madness was so terrible that it did not look as though it was going to die down. We watched while there was a real battle of wills and words and a tremendous shaking and pitching this way and that. And then suddenly the demons were out of the man and into the pigs. In the space of a few seconds we saw the pigs hurl themselves down the steep bank – hundreds of them[33] – and they plunged into the sea and drowned.

We had come for a rest and no incident could have been more exhausting. But the poor man was free of his madness and as quiet as a lamb, so we all shared something of his sense of peace. He was really a nice fellow, and as grateful as could be to Jesus. Since he had nothing on, and in his new sanity he was deeply embarrassed about it, the men among us saw what they were wearing that they could give him (you always had to be ready to shed your most intimate possessions when you were with Jesus). We also combed his hair and washed his face and dressed the wounds he had made on his body with the stones. Before anyone else arrived on the scene he was sitting down at Jesus' feet, fully clothed, along with the rest of us, the only odd thing being that he still had bits of chain hanging from his limbs – he would have to get a metal worker to release him from those.

The people who turned up had been summoned by those looking after the pigs. So there we were once again, surrounded by another crowd – it looked as though the whole of Gadara had come out to have a gape. You would think they would be grateful at being delivered from the dangerous lunatic, but then of course they had lost several hundred pigs, which had probably had rather a severe effect on their economy. In any case, they appeared to be as frightened now by the strange events as they must have been in the past by the madman's violence. They asked us to leave at once. It was rather awful really – not exactly a happy ending to the miracle.

The former madman begged to be allowed to come with us, but Jesus said no. It really would not have worked – he was a good chap but he was not even Jewish and he would have had too much to learn. Jesus left him in good heart, however. No one

∽

33 Two thousand of them according to Mark 5:13.

was ever rejected, they were just given different missions. And so he was sent away with a responsible task to fulfil – to spread the word of the great things God had done for him. (I learned some years later that the man had interpreted this in his own way, and had spread the word of the great things *Jesus* had done for him.)

And so it was back to Capernaum again, and back to the round of healings and teachings. Jesus healed the paralysed and the dumb, the blind and the bleeding, and he captivated the crowds with the vividness of his story-telling. Those who stayed on to express some kind of commitment found their consciences scoured by his soul-searching standards. Were we well-fed or well-off? Then we could expect a change of fortune. Were we happy or respected? Then it was more than we deserved. Had we wasted our gifts? Then we were fit to be trampled underfoot. Were we angry with another? Then we could expect God's anger. Did we swear? Then we were in the grip of the evil one. Did we resent being robbed? Then our allegiance was to our possessions more than to God. Were we unkind to our enemies? Then we were no true children of God. Were we kind to our friends and relatives? Then we deserved no praise at all. Did we allow others to know when we gave to charity? Then we had done nothing commendable. Had we criticized others? Then we were hypocrites. The gate is narrow, he told us, and the road is hard that leads to life. And there are few who find it.[34]

By the end of an evening's teaching I could often feel humbled and worthless, and yet I was never discouraged; rather I would yearn for a quality of goodness that I never possessed but which shone before me like a beacon on the path, enticing me with its pure light.

And there were indeed few who stayed on that narrow, hard path, for followers left almost as fast as they came. For every thousand who came to see and hear him, ten might show a lasting interest, and you were lucky if even one would really stay the course. And from the excitement and romance of the early work, the road became harder, and harder, and harder. The first major problem was that the crowds became such a pest. Often we could

---

34 Taken from the sermon on the mount, which was delivered to Jesus' disciples: Matthew 5:1 – 7:27.

not so much as sit down with a sandwich.[35] So we all became tired and hungry and run down. Jesus was not unreasonable about this – he said quite clearly we must get away and get some rest. But it often did not work out that way.

We went to southern Galilee, away from our more usual haunts, to Nain,[36] but such a crowd followed us that we found we were just spreading Jesus' reputation in yet another place. And then, as we came up to the city gates we met a funeral party, with a widow mourning the loss of her only son. Jesus could not see someone in a plight like that without being moved to pity and going forward to comfort her. He stopped the coffin and the next thing we knew was that the young man was not dead at all but was given alive and well to his mother. So then Jesus was even more mobbed by wondering and curious crowds.

Another time Jesus led a few of us way up to the north-east, into Phoenicia, near Tyre, with the firm intention of finding a place where nobody knew him. But even there he found he could not escape. A foreign woman came up to him crying out about her daughter who needed healing. Jesus tried to ignore her and we all told him to send her away, because she was drawing other people's attention to him, while we were trying to stay incognito. He was very torn: he tried to make it clear that he must have a break from time to time, and yet in the end of course he was swayed by compassion, and he healed the child. The result was entirely predictable: a couple of dozen others turned up in no time asking him to stop and help them.

Jesus seemed to draw on an absolutely inexhaustible spring of compassion, which left me feeling quite selfish in comparison. Once we had been besieged by the same crowd of four thousand for three days and nights on end, as Jesus helped one after another to walk, to see, to hear and to speak. Families would come and simply dump at our feet people with the most horrendous deformities. There they would lie in a pile, moaning and flailing, and it was a full-time job looking after them until their turn came, which might be some hours later. If any of us felt the occasional

---

35 'The crowd came together again, so that they could not even eat' (Mark 3:20). 'They had no leisure even to eat' (Mark 6:31).

36 The story is found in Luke 7:11–17.

stirring of revulsion Jesus did not. He could not rest so long as he saw people in genuine need, and he laid his hands on all of them, taking what time was needed to love them into life and fitness.

By the end of the third day we were completely exhausted, not to mention famished, but all Jesus could say was how sorry he felt for all *the crowd*, because *they* must be so tired and hungry. We could not resist pointing out that in that case they had the choice of going home – an option that was not open to us – but Jesus would not accept it. No, he said, they would faint on the journey back, and some had come a very long way. Then he made them all sit down on the ground. He took all the food we had, which was seven loaves and a few small fish, which he blessed and broke, and gave bits to each of us to take along the rows. At first I was handing out very small pieces, but every time I went back to Jesus he had more. Soon I began to realize there would be enough for me to have a nibble too as I handed it out. And then it seemed just to go on and on. In the end the same people were turning down the offer of more helpings, not because they were trying not to be greedy but because they were actually full. Then we began collecting up any leftovers, so we could redistribute them, but even after everyone had had enough we found we still had seven baskets full of scraps. Then at last Jesus sent away the crowd, confident that they were refreshed to make the journey home, and we got into our boat and crossed the lake to my own town of Magdala.[37]

I would have liked to stay there a while, but it did not work out that way. Jesus, who had such bottomless patience for those in real need, had no time for troublemakers and timewasters. A small group of Pharisees and Sadducees came up to him in Magdala – I knew them well, they were a clever set – and they challenged him to produce a sign so that they could see if he was genuine. Jesus of course had no interest in proving himself to anyone. If he performed a sign he did it in response to someone's need of healing, not to satisfy anyone's curiosity about his powers. He annoyed them by telling them they could not read the signs that were plain for all to see. 'You know how to read the weather', he said, 'Red at night, shepherds' delight; red in the morning, shepherds' warn-

⟨⟨⟩⟩

37 I am following Matthew 15:21 – 16:4 and Mark 7:24 – 8:13. Other textual variants for 'Magdala' are 'Magadan' and 'Dalmanutha', which, however, are identified with Magdala.

ing. So why can't you read the signs of the times? Only evil and immoral people keep on looking for proofs. You won't get your sign. The only sign you get will be the sign of Jonah.' That left me as baffled as the clever set, as Jesus swept us away out of Magdala to set sail once more.

Gradually he began to drop more clues about the 'sign of Jonah'. When we were alone together he started to tell us awful things that we did not want to listen to. He would have to go to Jerusalem, he said; he would have to suffer at the hands of the elders and chief priests and scribes; he would be killed; and on the third day he would rise again.[38] (Jonah had been in the body of the whale for three days, before being regurgitated onto the shore.) Peter told him to put such thoughts out of his head, for he had shown he was more than a match for any elders and scribes, and someone who could raise the widow of Nain's son from his coffin need not fall victim to the powers of death himself. Jesus turned on him suddenly with desperate fury and terrified us all with the violence of his language: 'Get behind me, Satan!' he shouted, 'These are human values you are presenting, not God's values!' From then on none of us ventured a query when he made the same warning again.[39] We were hurt and distressed and frightened and puzzled by what he said. But we did not dare question it.

By this time we were indeed on our way up to Jerusalem. And the atmosphere of foreboding was growing worse by the day. 'If you do not pick up your cross and carry it after me', Jesus told us, alluding even more explicitly to what was to turn out to be his method of execution, 'then you cannot be my follower.' And another time: 'Nobody builds a tower without estimating the cost first. Nobody goes to war without assessing the chances of defeat first. If you want to be my follower, you too must reckon on the cost. It will cost you everything that you have.' In the face of all these premonitions of disaster, another of our party dropped out as we set off for Judaea. 'I will follow you later on', he said as he

38 The first prophecy of the passion is found in Matthew 16:21–23, Mark 8:31–33 and Luke 9:22.

39 The second and third prophecy of the passion are found in Matthew 17:22–23, Mark 9:30–32 and Luke 9:43–45; Matthew 20:17–19, Mark 10:32–34 and Luke 18:31–34.

made his excuses, 'but first let me say goodbye to those at home.'
Jesus replied, 'No one who puts a hand to the plough and looks
back is fit for the reign of God.' Why did I stay with him on that
anxious journey, I and the other women from Galilee? Was it fear
of being reproved? No. It was love.[40]

And so we continued, coming closer to danger all the time.
Jesus led us on, like a beacon of light in the dark of night, and the
more hostile the surroundings, the more audaciously his light
shone. He told story after story, matching them to his listeners.
When he was with people of weak morals he told welcoming and
encouraging stories about shepherds looking for lost sheep, or
women looking for lost coins. When he was with us, his committed
followers, he told stories that challenged and increasingly alarmed
us about the obligations of stewards to invest well and stay attentive at every moment, and the punishments awaiting us if we did
not live up to the high standards demanded. And when he was with

---

40 So far I have attempted to recreate the kind of experiences Mary of
Magdala might have had in the Galilee period as she travelled with
Jesus. We do know that she travelled with him in Galilee: see note
24 on p. 124 above, even though we are not told explicitly that she
was present on any of the occasions mentioned. (The sayings in this
paragraph come from Luke 14:27–33 and Luke 9:61–62.)

I have chosen to follow this method in order to do what Carla
Ricci describes as 'questioning the silence'. She points out that, at the
miracles of the loaves, Matthew speaks of '5,000 men, besides women
and children' (Matthew 14:21) and '4,000 men, besides women and
children' (Matthew 15:38), where the other gospels only say '5,000
men' (or '4,000 men'). From this she concludes: 'The providentiality
of this annotation in Matthew's text is that it implies that it is
methodologically legitimate to explore: every time the writings are
silent about women and do not mention their presence it will be quite
unfounded to deduce their absence. One can rather question the
silence, the unspoken, the unwritten, the unrecorded, the tradition
that has not been handed down' (*Maria di Magdala e le Molte Altre*,
pp. 20–1).

Some task of hypothetical reconstruction was badly needed, if
we were to get a plausible idea of what the women might have
witnessed, so I have spent some time over this quite deliberately.
From this point on, however, we are able to rejoin the more explicit
trail of the gospels – the passion, which all the evangelists tell us Mary
Magdalene witnessed, and the resurrection likewise.

rich and smug Pharisees, he told accusing stories about a rich man ignoring a beggar at his gate and going to hell for it, or about a proud upright man and a humble sinner praying in the temple, and the sinner being more pleasing to God.[41]

And all the time the warnings were increasing, while Jesus strode on defiantly. From then on it was as though I was stumbling down a dark tunnel. All that kept me going was the blinding light at the far end, which was Jesus, always drawing me after him. I had little understanding of why he had chosen this path of confrontation, though I trusted that what he did was right, whatever the consequences.

We women grew very close in those days, as we huddled together for courage. Hand in hand, or arm in arm, we followed him now in silence – I and the other Mary, Joanna and Susanna and Salome. Gone were the Galilean days of confident ministry and happy partnership. I felt all activity, all thought, all planning, all initiative was drained out of me, and I had strength only to trail behind, borne along by the support of my sisters in the gospel.

Together we walked behind him over the cobbles, like a sad and subdued royal retinue, as he entered Jerusalem on the back of a donkey, while the crowd bayed, 'Blessed is the king who comes in the name of God.' Our hearts were turning over with fear and trepidation, while the people shouted and whooped for joy. Jesus wept with anguish, and we were close enough to hear him cry, 'If

41 In Luke, the parables of the lost sheep and lost coin are told to a group that includes tax collectors and sinners (Luke 15:1–10).

The teaching about selling your possessions and giving alms, together with the parable of the burglary and the drunken servants, are spoken to the disciples in private (Luke 12:22, 35–48), calling forth the question of Peter, 'Are you telling this parable for us or for everyone?' (Luke 12:41). (This is even clearer in Matthew, where the parables of the burglary, the drunken servants, the ten virgins and the talents, Matthew 24:43 – 25:46, are all told to the group of disciples in private before Jesus enters Jerusalem, Matthew 24:3.)

The parable of the rich man and the beggar is told to 'Pharisees, who were lovers of money' (Luke 16:14, 19–31), while the parable of the two men praying in the temple is told to 'some who trusted in themselves that they were righteous and regarded others with contempt' (Luke 18:9–14).

only you had recognized on this day the things that make for peace.'[42]

Together we walked behind him up the steps to the temple, and meekly watched him overthrowing tables and chairs and yelling at the stall-holders that they had turned God's house of prayer into a den of thieves. Jesus threw himself about this way and that, banging and arguing, as we stood to the side like a bunch of stupid dummies. Then together we turned and followed him out again.

Together we returned to the temple and stood at his side as we heard him preaching against the priests and elders. He told them that prostitutes would go to heaven before them. He likened them to murderers, who set upon their landlord's only son and killed him. And he told them they were like a man at a wedding feast who had not bothered to dress for the occasion: he would be bound hand and foot and thrown into the outer darkness, where there was weeping and gnashing of teeth.[43] The Pharisees and elders were white with anger. Each time we went into the temple we were afraid we would not emerge again safely.

Joanna was a help on those occasions, for her experience in Herod's court had given her a self-confidence that made her walk tall and free. Salome was another support: as a mother of two adult sons who were among the twelve,[44] her commitment to Jesus was very solid. And the other Mary was the one who most often put her arm around me to give me courage. And so we bore each other up.

42 For the entry into Jerusalem, we are following Luke 19:38ff.

43 In this paragraph we change over to Matthew's parallel account of the last days of preaching in the temple (Matthew 21:23 – 22:13).

44 We might hypothesize that Salome was 'the mother of the sons of Zebedee', by comparing the parallel texts of Matthew and Mark concerning the women watching the crucifixion: 'Among them were Mary Magdalene, and Mary the mother of James and Joseph, and the mother of the sons of Zebedee' (Matthew 27:56). 'Among them were Mary Magdalene, and Mary the mother of James the younger and of Joses, and Salome' (Mark 15:40).

Together we stood in the thick of the crowd outside Pilate's palace after the arrest on that fateful Friday, a small besieged island of speechlessness amid a sea of hostile voices. Together we waited outside the exit from the cells, knowing that sooner or later the condemned must pass this way on the path to execution. Together we saw the prisoners come out in chains, and the third and last was Jesus, looking terrible after his scourging. Together we stepped into the procession behind him, to follow the king who had come in the name of God. We walked the cobbled streets to the gate of the city, as we had walked them in the other direction just a few days earlier. The crowd bayed again around us, but with jeering, not cheering.

We were like so many women the world over, who have followed the men they loved along the path of suffering – crying and grieving and sharing in their shame. Many women have no choice but to do so: we had a choice, for there was another route we could have taken. We could have copied the twelve who had escaped to safety. Of course they were in serious risk of arrest, which we were not: who would bother to arrest a bunch of women? If our sex at times made us invisible, on this occasion it gave us a certain protection, though what we did was still undoubtedly dangerous.[45]

I felt useless on that journey to Calvary, and yet later I understood how much we had done by our passive following. We had kept the continuity of the Church alive in its moment of greatest crisis and destruction. The men, who later handed on accounts of Jesus' life, and who tended in most situations to speak as though we were not even present, were compelled to mention us at that point, because there was no one else whom they could mention.[46] Without us women – doing nothing, saying nothing,

45 Ben Witherington's book presents the evidence for his conclusion that the women's open grieving was 'a spontaneous show of their feelings, but it was also a dangerous one, for the Jews did not permit such public crying and wailing for a criminal' (*Women in the Ministry of Jesus*, p. 49).

46 Matthew's first mention of the group of women followers is at the crucifixion, when he admits that this hitherto unmentioned group had been with Jesus ever since the ministry in Galilee: 'Many women were

but simply following – there would have been no constant thread between the community of Jesus' followers before his death and after his rising. When the men failed, we kept the light of faith alight.

And I remembered the story Jesus told about ten virgins who took their lamps and waited for the bridegroom to come.[47] Five ran out of oil and had to go to buy some more, so they missed the moment they had been waiting for; but the other five had enough oil to see them through, and were there ready and waiting when the bridegroom arrived. It was as though the men were the five virgins who had run out of oil, because they found they had not the resources to stay with Jesus at the hour of his arrest. But we women were the virgins with enough oil to see us through the long night and to be with Jesus at his time of greatest need.

And then we found we were not alone, for another group of women was coming to meet us along the road, like ministering angels sent to reinforce and strengthen us. They were not from Galilee, but rather were women who had been won over by Jesus here in Jerusalem. And their cries and tears made clear that they were putting themselves on the side of Jesus, even in his condemnation. We were consoled by their support, and Jesus was so touched that he stopped in his grinding passage up the hill and found the words to speak to them with great affection. 'Daughters of Jerusalem', he said, 'do not cry for me.' But they cried the more, as we did too. He said again, 'Do not cry for me, but if you must cry, cry for yourselves, and cry for your children. There are terrible days lying ahead, and people will wish they had never been born. If this is what they do to me, then what will they do to others after

also there, looking on from a distance; they had followed Jesus from Galilee and had provided for him. Among them were Mary Magdalene, and Mary the mother of James and Joseph, and the mother of the sons of Zebedee' (Matthew 27:55–56). Mark, too, only mentions them at this point (Mark 15:40), and so does John (John 19:25). Only Luke, with his brief verses at the start of chapter 8, has given us prior notification of the fact that there were women who followed Jesus on his travels.

47 The parable of the wise and foolish virgins is in Matthew 25:1–13.

me?'[48] And then we carried on up the hill, women from Galilee and Jerusalem walking together and weeping together, and Jesus staggering on ahead of us.

At the place of execution they nailed him to a cross and there was nothing for us to do, absolutely nothing, except watch.[49] I was praying my heart out, 'O God, if there is anything I can do for him, then let me do it. If I can bear any of his pain to relieve him a little, then let me bear it. If I can die instead of him, then let me die. I give him to you, O God, we all give him to you. We sacrifice him to you. Take him quickly. Only spare him the pain, I beg you, spare him the pain.'

And then I saw with horror that Mary, his mother, was there. I do not know how long she had been with us, for I had not noticed her before, so engrossed had I been in my own grief. And I knew that however bad it was for me to stand and watch, it was ten times worse for a mother. It was the other Mary who alerted me; she whispered, 'Look, there's his mother. Do you think we should take her away?' But I knew that that would be a far worse cruelty. We all had to be faithful and to see it through to the end, whatever it cost us. So I went and took her in my arms, and held her up, and she was as limp and lifeless as a leaf in autumn, with glazed eyes transfixed on him.

But it was so long. I cannot tell you how long that afternoon was.

Just before dusk he died, and they took down his body. It was not him any more, he was gone, but it was all we had left of him. Joseph of Arimathea and Nicodemus,[50] both of whom I mentioned earlier, had turned up, and they helped us take down the body, and wrap it in a cloth that Joseph had brought with him. We had to rush now, for it would be dark very shortly and that

48 It is Luke who gives us the account of the daughters of Jerusalem following Jesus as he carried his cross (Luke 23:27–31).

49 According to Matthew, Mark and Luke, Mary of Magdala was watching from afar; according to John 19:25 she was standing with Jesus' mother beside the cross.

50 Joseph of Arimathea is recorded in all four gospels at this point, but Nicodemus is mentioned only in John 19:39.

would be the start of the sabbath, when all activity would be at an end for 24 hours. Joseph and Nicodemus were marvellous: they had arranged a nearby tomb, and when we had hurriedly lugged the body there they leant their combined weights against the stone and sealed the entrance, just as the sun set. We had not had time to anoint the body, which we all wanted very badly to do as a sign of our overwhelming love, but at least the body would be safe until Sunday morning when we could return with spices and ointments prepared.

Joseph left, and so did Nicodemus, and then the other women went, including Jesus' mother. But the other Mary and I stayed on in the gathering darkness, sitting over against the tomb,[51] and staring at the entrance stone, until we could no longer make it out, and thinking of what was inside and what we had seen that day. We did not speak for a long time, until at last the other Mary said, 'I'm getting cold. Do you think we should go back now?', and we picked our way, very slowly in the dark, over the stony ground towards the city beneath.

Saturday was a dead day, in every sense. I sat inside in the house where we were staying, and looked at the wall all day long, just as the night before I had sat outside and looked at the tomb-stone. I found it a relief that it was the sabbath: I could not have coped with doing anything. We were all in a state of numbness and no one felt like talking.

The men, who had come to join us in the house, were cowed and frightened, depressed and despairing. They sat in another room and were too ashamed as yet even to ask for details of the death. Joanna and Susanna went out to get spices and ointments: I do not know where they got them from on the sabbath, but they had very good contacts. The rest of us just kept still and quiet while our minds went over and over the horrific scenes, beginning the long and demanding mental work of slowly absorbing and process-ing the memories. You will ask, 'What did we think? Did we have faith? Did we think it was the end?' But you do not think at a time like that. There is no spare mental energy for thoughts. The mind is taken up with memories, larger than life memories, re-running their course over and over.

---

51 Joseph of Arimathea went away, while 'Mary Magdalene and the other Mary were there, sitting opposite the tomb' (Matthew 27:60–61).

I slept fitfully both nights, and woke very early on the Sunday. I slipped out alone[52] while it was still dark, to go back to the tomb. Just as I had seen the stone fade into invisibility in the blackness on Friday night, I thought I would wait and see it re-emerge into light as dawn broke. I wanted to be there, waiting, until eventually the others would come and we would move the stone and embalm the body.

I reached the tomb with some difficulty, for I had no light to pick my way, and I was not very familiar with the route. I sat down as I had before, and waited for the dawn. I could not understand why the entrance looked so dark, but I thought as the light came I would make sense of the shadows. As the sky lightened, the black and grey world of night slowly began to pick up traces of colour. But what puzzled me was this: I could not make out the stone at all. Gradually horror edged its way into my awareness, as I first wondered, then suspected, then was nearly sure, and finally could see without a shadow of doubt that there was no stone at the entrance at all. Indeed I could now see quite clearly that it had been moved away: it was rolled to the side. And worse than that, there was no reassuring bump of body within: the white sheet lay flatly on the shelf. There was no doubt about it: the body had gone.

After so long sitting and waiting I suddenly jumped up and ran, as panic overtook me. I ran across the scrub, onto the path, down to the road, through the city gates, and along the streets – which were just beginning to stir into life – until I came to the house. 'They have taken Jesus' body out of the tomb, and I don't know where they have put him', I panted. Peter was up and out in a flash, with another one of the men. I did not want to be left behind, so I ran back after them, without having time to tell the news to the others.

I wanted to be with the two men when they found the empty

52 Although Matthew, Mark and Luke record that Mary went to the tomb in the company of the other women (the other Mary, plus Salome in Mark, and Joanna and others in Luke), I have followed instead the account in the fourth gospel (John 20: 1–18), as it is by far the richest record of Mary Magdalene's experiences on that morning. Note that Mark (in the longer ending) records that Jesus 'appeared first to Mary Magdalene' (Mark 16: 9).

tomb. But I could not keep up. I fell far behind, partly because they could run so much faster than me, and partly because I was already out of breath, and the way back was uphill. I strained to catch up but it was useless. My heart was pounding and my lungs burning. I had to slow down, and walk, running only in short fits and starts. They were miles ahead. I struggled back to the tomb again and found no sign of them. They had gone, without even telling me where they were going or what they were doing about the theft of the body. I stood outside the tomb, and I wept.

I do not know how long passed, but my sobs were so loud and so shook my body that I can even now remember their noisiness in that still and tranquil morning. After all the trauma of the last two days, and after all the anxiety of several months before that, it was as though at last my defences broke right down and anguish broke over me in great waves. I held my veil to my face to soak up my tears and to blow my nose into, and soon it was a damp rag sodden from end to end. I had nothing to lose now, nothing, not even the corpse, all was gone. My life – which had been so painstakingly remade out of its former chaos – lay once more in ruins about my feet. Nothing made sense any more, nor did I have any hope that it ever would make sense again.

I stooped and looked in the tomb again at the empty shelf. Through my watery eyes I could now make out two men sitting there, dressed in white, one at either end of where the body had been laid. They spoke to me, 'Woman, why are you crying?' I was too distressed to wonder who they were or where they came from, and I blurted out, 'Because they have taken away Jesus, and I do not know where they have put him.'

I turned my swollen, blubbing eyes away from them, but found instead someone had come up on the other side. I thought it must be the gardener. He asked me the same question, 'Woman, why are you crying? Who are you looking for?' I tried to pull myself together, for I thought he might be the one who had moved the body. 'Sir', I said, trying to steady my voice, 'If you have carried him away, tell me where you have laid him, and I will take him away.' He said to me, 'Mary!'

Something stirred in me like a primeval memory. Was it my mother, calling me by name as a baby? Was it even before that, as God called me out of nothingness into creation? There was a moment when I was called in this way before . . . and now I had it: I was leaving the synagogue in my home town of Magdala, when someone called me back, and the name of 'Mary' seemed to come from my own heart, it felt so close to me.[53]

As in Magdala, I turned. And as in Magdala my life changed in that turning around. I turned from doubt to faith, from fear to joy, from grief to ecstasy. I turned my back on a life of darkness and confusion and faced the new life of light[54] and purity in the world where God reigns. I turned and looked my saviour in the face, blinking away my tears to see him more clearly. I knelt then, humbled, grateful, reverent, wondering, and spoke to him in a single word, by which I meant so much: 'Rabbi!'

I was saying, 'I believe.' I was saying, 'Jesus, my Messiah, you have risen from the dead.' I was saying, 'Now you have taught me everything.' I was saying, 'My joy is boundless.' I was saying, 'I will devote my whole life to you, and have no other God before you.' I was saying, 'I love you.' I was saying so much more than can be put into words, but which is the task of a whole lifetime to explore. 'Mary!' 'Rabbi!' I had no desire to say another word.

Jesus was standing right before me as I knelt, and I stretched out my hand to touch him. He was as warm and real as I had ever known him, and I would have thrown both arms around his legs to clasp him to me had he not caught my hand and gently disentangled himself. 'Don't hold on to me', he told me, 'Let me ascend to God first.'[55] And I saw then that his hand was wounded

53 In Mary's recognition of Jesus when he calls her by name there are echoes of John 10: 3–4: 'He calls his own sheep by name and leads them out. When he has brought out all his own he goes ahead of them, and the sheep follow him because they know his voice.'

54 Mary Magdalene makes widespread use of the metaphor of light in this chapter. Light was a similarly powerful image for the fourth evangelist, especially in his Prologue: 'The light shines in darkness, and the darkness did not overcome it' (John 1: 5). See also note 29 on p. 73.

55 Lilia Sebastiani produces the fascinating information that 'some near-contemporaries of ours have had the nerve to suggest that Jesus at that moment must have been naked (if his funeral shroud had remained in the tomb) and for that reason it was most inconvenient

– with a hole where the nail had passed through – though it seemed to cause him no pain.[56] Jesus said to me, 'Go back to my brothers. Go and tell them what you have seen. Tell them that I said, "I am ascending to my God and your God".'[57] So Jesus had not changed: he never sent anyone away without giving them their own mission, their own message to take to others.[58]

But what a mission, what a message![59] Never before had anyone had the task of bearing the news that the Messiah had risen from the dead! And I, who was a woman, was sent to teach the men! I rose to my feet to show I was ready to go at his command, but first we looked at each other, hard and long, tracing with our

that a woman should embrace him' (*Tra/Sfigurazione*, p. 19). She considers nine possible interpretations of the difficult phrase 'Do not touch/hold onto me', and concludes that it is perhaps not inappropriate that these words should be shrouded in a certain mystery (pp. 273–6). My own rendering suggests that just as the disciples had to let go of Jesus as he went to his death (see John 13:36 and 14:28), so too they had to let go of him as he rose to his full glory in the Ascension.

56 John gives us this detail at Jesus' next appearance, a few verses on in the same gospel (John 20:20, 25–26).

57 Remembering the long conversation with the woman at the well from John 4, Elisabeth Moltmann-Wendel reflects that John had a 'predilection for extended conversations between Jesus and women' (*The Women Around Jesus*, p. 70).

58 For the way Jesus sends people away with a mission of their own, see Mark 5:19, Luke 8:39, as well as p. 132 above.

59 In medieval legend Mary Magdalene extends her mission of preaching to Provence, where it was alleged she had gone, with her spiritual director Maximinus, after being exiled from Palestine. As the legend developed she became detached from Maximinus, and began an evangelizing ministry of her own, and she is seen preaching in a thirteenth-century stained glass window in the great church of Semur in Burgundy. Such legends were common (see also Photina: note 2 on p. 54, and Martha and Mary of Bethany: note 1 on p. 78) and they are unlikely to have any historical foundation.

eyes every loved detail of the other's face. This was the same Jesus in every way, and yet different. How can I describe it? He looked more free than before, with every shade of anxiety gone from his brow. He looked more radiant, and yet not a trace ethereal. He looked more life-giving, more healthy, even (as odd as it sounds) more physical. I felt no worry at all now that he would be lost from me or fade away irrecoverably. Had he not come to me when I needed him? Could I not trust that he would always be there for me now, not perhaps whenever I wanted him, but certainly whenever I needed him?

That moment was precious, and as brief as it was it held a sort of infinity within it. And I dare to say that the moment of my meeting with the risen Jesus has become precious to others too. For as I tell my story to others I see them taken up into my experience; I see them imagining themselves there in my place, turning at the sound of their name, turning to meet Jesus, turning with their own cry of 'Rabbi!' I was the first, the very first,[60] to see him again alive, and yet a myriad of witnesses came to share the resurrection faith through me. Jesus did not only come to me because I needed to see him, but because the Church needed to see him through me.

And then, with joy we both went on our different missions. He went to God, to receive the fullness of his risen glory. And I went to humanity, to share with them the good news. Never has news been so good, for this was good news not just

60 On this point, that Mary of Magdala was the first witness to the resurrection, there is general agreement. Matthew places her first, together with the other Mary, in seeing the risen Christ (Matthew 28:1, 9). Mark, in the longer ending, tells us that Jesus 'appeared first to Mary Magdalene' (Mark 16:9). In Luke she is together with Joanna, Mary the mother of James, and the other women, in being first witness to the empty tomb, even if the first appearance of Jesus in person is not clearly recorded. (The appearance at Emmaus, Luke 24:31, though it is the first appearance mentioned, does not appear to be the first appearance chronologically, see 24:34.) Paul, however, in 1 Corinthians 15:5–8, omits all mention of the women as resurrection witnesses, including Mary Magdalene, and only records the appearances to men – to Cephas (that is, Peter), to the twelve, to five hundred brothers (or brothers and sisters, the Greek could mean either), to James, to all the apostles (this appears to be a different group from the twelve, previously mentioned), and finally to Paul himself.

for me, not just for the sisters and brothers in the house, not just for all the Christians alive today, but for all people, everywhere, and for all time. Because Jesus lives, we too may live with new life, and death shall be no more. And I was entrusted with that news, so good and precious and beautiful that it was like sweet honey dripping in the mouth, or like fine gold glowing in the sand, or like a tiny baby nestling in the arms of its mother.[61]

I returned to the house and told the twelve the good news. I said, 'I have seen Jesus.' And they did not believe me.[62] I told them what he had said, that he had given me the message, 'I am ascending to my God and your God.' And they looked at me as men often look at a woman, as people who think they know everything look at someone who they think knows nothing. Poor them. I knew, and they did not. Nothing could shake them from the dreadful despair they clung to, but nothing could take from me the boundless joy that had set me free.[63]

This is how it came about that I, who had begun as a sick woman in need of healing, grew in such love and devotion to Jesus that he chose me to be apostle to the apostles.[64] And this is how

61 I have made Mary speak in a way that is evocative of scriptural references about the beauty of God's word: 'The ordinances of the Lord are true and righteous altogether. More to be desired are they than gold,' even much fine gold; sweeter also than honey, and drippings of the honeycomb' (Psalm 19:9–10). 'You shall nurse and be carried on her arm, and dandled on her knees. As a mother comforts her child, so I will comfort you' (Isaiah 66:12–13).

62 'But when they heard that he was alive and had been seen by her, they would not believe it' (Mark 16:11). David Friedrich Strauss, in the nineteenth century, must have thought they were quite right not to believe it, when he mocked a Christianity based on the 'visions of a half-crazy woman'.

63 These feelings echo the words of Jesus, 'You have pain now, but I will see you again, and your hearts will rejoice, and no one will take your joy from you' (John 16:22).

64 This is a traditional and accepted title for Mary of Magdala, used for example by Bernard of Clairvaux (*Sermones in Canticum, Serm.* 75,

it came about that even those commissioned by God can see their work come to nothing, and their attempts to serve the Church rendered fruitless, because they are women. I look forward in joy to the day when the Church will open her ears in greater faith to hear the good news proclaimed by women, so that the intention of Jesus may be more fully realized. May that day come speedily.[65]

8: PL 183, 1148) and by Rabanus Maurus: *Salvator . . . ascensionis suae eam [Mariam Magdalenam] ad apostolos instituit apostolam*, 'The Saviour commissioned her [Mary Magdalene] as apostle to the apostles [with the news] of his ascension' (*De vita beatae Mariae Magdalenae*, XXVII: PL 112, 1474). Thomas Aquinas, too, calls her 'apostle of the apostles': *Facta est Apostolorum Apostola per hoc quod ei committitur ut resurrectionem dominicam discipulis annuntiet*, 'She has been made Apostle of the Apostles by virtue of what is entrusted to her, that she should announce the resurrection of the Lord to the disciples' (*In Joannem Evangelistam Expositio*, c. XX, L. III, 6, *Sancti Thomae Aquinatis Comment. in Matthaeum et Joannem Evangelistas*, ed. Parmens. X, 629).

It may be noted that for Paul, the term apostle is not restricted to the twelve: not only does he call himself an apostle repeatedly, but he speaks also of Andronicus and Junia as 'prominent among the apostles' (Romans 16:7). (Junia may well be a woman. since the noun is feminine in form.) According to Lilia Sebastiani: 'for Paul, the dignity and mission of the apostle is based on having seen the risen Lord. . . . Adopting the Pauline criteria, we would have to admit that no one is an apostle to the extent that Mary of Magdala is: she was first to see Jesus risen, she recognized him when she was called by him by name (the characteristic of the true disciple according to John), and she was charged with taking the news of the resurrection – the basis for every subsequent proclamation of the good news – to the group of the Eleven, while they were still prey to incredulity and fear' (*Tra/Sfigurazione*, p. 46).

65 'That day' is a term used by Paul to refer to the day of the second coming of Christ, when 'the work of each builder will become visible' (1 Corinthians 3:13), and 'the crown of righteousness' be awarded to those who deserve it for their work (2 Timothy 4:8). It is an appropriate term to focus the aspirations of women for a day when their work may stand on equal terms with that of men.

CONCLUSION

'Who is the greatest?' is not a Christian question, but it is one which we find hard not to slip into on occasions. As we enter into the lives of these six remarkable women, we are amazed at the hidden significance of their actions. We cannot help noticing that the twelve male apostles appear, not diminished, but relativized in comparison with what these women have achieved.

After all, apart from Peter, Judas and the beloved disciple – who may or may not have been one of the twelve – we have very little idea of the characters or individuality of the apostles. James and John tag along with Peter on a number of occasions, but some of the others only ever appear in a list.

With these women from the gospels, however, it is easier to uncover vivid character studies of six highly individual and significant figures. They stand as models and patrons for preachers, priests and theologians, as we explore the multiple ways in which they interpreted and proclaimed the faith by word and act. And we can even find ourselves wondering which of the six women is the greatest.

A good candidate would be Elizabeth, the generous, devoted, priestly woman who, tested by years of waiting, was the first to make a Christological acclamation, prophetically sensing even what was hidden in the womb.

Or should we choose the practical, hard-working, outspoken Martha, whose profession of faith, at the end of Jesus' ministry, paralleled more closely that made by Peter, the leader of the twelve?

But then what about the highly-sexed Photina? Though she strategically masks her belief in question form – 'Could this be the Messiah?' – she becomes Jesus' first apostle, of either sex, beyond his own nation. She is truly a pioneer.

These three women were quite outstanding. And yet the three Marys shine out with a brilliance even beyond theirs.

There is Mary of Nazareth, who apparently gave Jesus all his genes. She shaped his human development as a child, and shared with him nine-tenths of his life. Her pondered memories have rescued the incarnation from an abstract intellectual idea and turned it into a lived human reality. Her story has such a theological richness and complexity that it is capable of endless development. She is the one whom the Church has traditionally recognized as the greatest of all women, and the greatest of all disciples.

Yet today it is Mary of Magdala whose role we recognize with increasing clarity, rescuing her from the slander of centuries. As Mary of Nazareth faded from view in Jesus' public ministry, Mary of Magdala stepped forward into a leadership role. She was the evangelists' choice as pre-eminent woman disciple, and she was Jesus' choice as first Easter witness. It is fitting that her story forms the closing climax of this book.

But Mary of Bethany performed an act that, arguably, makes her the most important figure of all. She anointed Jesus as the Christ. He was the anointed one of God, but it was her hand that poured the oil. It was her deed that launched him into the paschal mysteries of suffering, death and resurrection. No wonder Jesus declared that what she did was part of the essential core of the faith, to be retold throughout the world in her honour.

A mother of a prisoner, a woman flustered by housework, a heretic five times divorced. . . . An unmarried mother, a former mental patient, an extravagant dreamer. . . . What an unlikely bunch Jesus chose to be witnesses to the truth! And so in the end we come back to Jesus' own answer to the question, 'Who is the greatest?' He replied, 'The least among you all is the one who is greatest' (Luke 9:48).

After two millennia of Christian history, in which women have been silent and invisible, and even today are widely considered unfit for priestly ministry, one cannot help feeling that Jesus was right.

BIBLIOGRAPHY

References have been made in the notes to works by Augustine, Bernard, Clement, Jerome, John Chrysostom, Josephus, Origen, Pliny, Rabanus Maurus, Teresa of Avila and Thomas Aquinas. In addition, there are references to the following modern works:

Dominique Barbé, *Grace and Power* (Orbis, New York, 1987).

Stephen C. Barton, 'Mark as narrative: the story of the anointing woman, Mk 14:3–9', *The Expository Times*, vol. 102, no. 8 (May 1991).

John N. Collins, *Diakonia: Reinterpreting the Ancient Sources* (Oxford University Press, 1992).

Henri Daniel-Rops, *La vie quotidienne en Palestine au temps de Jésus* (Hachette, Paris, 1961).

Eamon Duffy, *What Catholics Believe About Mary* (Catholic Truth Society, London, 1989).

Hilda Graef, *Mary: A History of Doctrine and Devotion* (Sheed and Ward, New York, 1963).

Aloys Grillmeier, *Christ in Christian Tradition*, vol. 1 (John Knox Press, Atlanta/Mowbray, London and Oxford, 1975).

Joachim Jeremias, *Jerusalem in the Time of Jesus* (Fortress Press, Philadelphia, 1969).

Joachim Jeremias, *The Prayers of Jesus* (Studies in Biblical Theology, second series, 6; SCM, London, 1967).

Alec McCowen, *Personal Mark* (Collins Fount, London, 1984).

Mary T. Malone, *Who Is My Mother? Rediscovering the Mother of Jesus* (Wm C. Brown Co., Iowa, 1984).

J. Massyngbaerde Ford, *My Enemy Is My Guest: Jesus and Violence in Luke* (Orbis, New York, 1984).

Elisabeth Moltmann-Wendel, *The Women Around Jesus*, trans. John Bowden (SCM, London/Crossroad, New York, 1982).

Janet Morley, *Beforehand for the Burial: A Quiet Day for Holy Week, Monday April 1st 1985* (Women in Theology, London, 1985).

Nag Hammadi Library in English, ed. James M. Robinson et al. (Harper and Row, New York, 1977).

New Jerusalem Bible (Darton Longman & Todd, London, 1985).

Jaroslav Pelikan (ed.), Commentary on the *Magnificat* in *Luther's Works*, vol. 21 (St Louis, 1956).

Carla Ricci, *Maria di Magdala e le Molte Altre* (M. d'Auria Editore, Naples, 1991).

Christopher Rowland, 'How the poor can liberate the Bible', *Priests and People* (London, October 1992).

Jane Schaberg, *The Illegitimacy of Jesus: A Feminist Theological Interpretation of the Infancy Narratives* (Harper and Row, 1987).

Elisabeth Schüssler Fiorenza, *But She Said: Feminist Practices of Biblical Interpretation* (Beacon Press, Boston, 1992).

Elisabeth Schüssler Fiorenza, *In Memory of Her: A Feminist Theological Reconstruction of Christian Origins* (Crossroad, New York/SCM, London, 1983).

Lilia Sebastiani, *Tra/Sfigurazione* (Queriniana, Brescia, 1992).

E. Stauffer, *Jesus and His Story*, trans. R. and C. Winston (Alfred A. Knopf, New York, 1974).

R. S. Sugirtharajah (ed.), *Voices from the Third World: Interpreting the Bible in the Third World* (SPCK, London, 1991).

Eva Catafygiotu Topping, *Holy Mothers of Orthodoxy: Women and the Church* (Light and Life Publishing Company, Minneapolis, Minnesota, 1987).

Eva Catafygiotu Topping, *Saints and Sisterhood: The Lives of Forty-Eight Holy Women: A Menologion or Month-by-Month Listing and Study of Women Saints on the Orthodox Calendar* (Light and Life, 1990).

Rachel Conrad Wahlberg, *Jesus According to a Woman* (Paulist, 1975; rev. edn 1986).

Barbara G. Walker, *The Crone: Woman of Age, Wisdom and Power* (HarperCollins, 1985).

Robert McL. Wilson (trans. and comm.), *Gospel of Philip* (Mowbray, London and Oxford, 1962).

Ben Witherington III, *Women in the Ministry of Jesus* (Cambridge University Press, 1984).

Women's Bible Commentary, ed. Carol A. Newsom and Sharon H. Ringe (SPCK, London, 1992).